CLEAN PLATES

N.Y.C.

A Guide to the Healthiest
Tastiest Restaurants
in Manhattan
for Vegetarians
and Carnivores

By JARED KOCH
Reviews by ALEX VAN BUREN

DISCLAIMER: I am not a medical doctor, and nothing in this book is intended to diagnose, treat or cure any medical condition, illness or disease. Anyone with a specific medical condition should consult a physician.

Published by Craving Wellness
West New York, NJ

Cover design by Jessica Arana
Interior design by Gary Robbins

Printed in the United States of America

10 9 8 7 6 5 4 3 2

Mixed Sources
Product group from well-managed forests and other controlled sources
www.fsc.org   Cert no. SW-COC-002283
© 1996 Forest Stewardship Council
FSC

*Library of Congress
Cataloging-in-Publication Data:*

Koch, Jared.
  Clean Plates NYC : a guide to the
  healthiest tastiest restaurants in
  Manhattan for vegetarians and
  carnivores / by Jared Koch ; with
  reviews by Alex Van Buren. – West New
  York, NJ : Craving Wellness, 2009.
  p.   cm.
  ISBN 978-0-9821862-0-6
  1. Food—Popular works.
  2. Diet—Popular works.
  3. Nutrition—Popular works.
  4. Restaurants—New York (State)
      —New York.
  I. Title.
  II. Van Buren, Alex.
TX355.K63   2009
641—dc22
2008940260

CONTENTS

ACKNOWLEDGMENTS

My deepest gratitude, appreciation and respect to the following people, without whom this book would not exist:

To all the chefs and restaurant owners dedicated to serving delicious but healthier food. A special thanks to Dan Barber, Bill Telepan, Sarma Mengalis, Debbie Covenagh, Amy Chaplin, Rene Duran, Melissa O'Donnell and Michael Anthony for taking the time to be interviewed.

Alex Van Buren for her talents, integrity and great dinner conversation. Angela Starks and Bunny Wong for all their help writing and editing the nutritional content. Pervaiz Shallwani for writing the chef interviews.

Jessica Arana for designing the logo and the book cover. Gary Robbins for interior design and layout. The whole gang at Monaco Lange for all of their invaluable suggestions.

Special thanks to Blake Appleby, my life partner, for always supporting, encouraging and inspiring me and offering her insightful opinions. To all my family, friends, teachers and clients who have contributed and enriched my life in so many significant ways. Greg Monaco for his talents, perspective and calm demeanor and for his invaluable advice every step of the way.

And to Mat Zucker, Lynnda Pollio, Yvonne Roehler at Jenkins Group, Kate Basrat, Ameet Maturu, Susan Banzon, Amy Bush, Angela Davis, Chad Thompson, Sam Rosen at ThoughtLead, Peter Horjus, Vera Svezia, Barry Flemming, Jeremy Funston, Lisa Vasher, Catherine Cusamano, Mark Sclafani, Katherine Jamieson, Kathleen Spinelli, Erin Turner, Michael Ellisberg, Nancy Weiser, Carey Peters, Brett Lavender, Cassandra Caffaltas, Kim Blozie and especially Andrew Cohen and everyone at EnlightenNext.

A NOTE FROM JARED

EATING HEALTHIER DOES NOT have to be challenging. Especially in Manhattan. Especially with this book. In fact, it can be an easy, pleasurable and sacrifice-free adventure. I've created this book for you—for New Yorkers and for visitors to this great city—with exactly that in mind.

Let's face it: We dine out a lot. And restaurants can be bad-eating minefields. Then again, who would say no if a delicious antibiotic and hormone-free steak or a plate of tasty organic vegetables materialized in front of them? No one actually *wants* to consume hormones, antibiotics or pesticides. It's just that searching for the good stuff takes time. Fortunately, it's been done for you, and with a one-two punch: Every featured selection in *Clean Plates NYC* is a restaurant that offers both delicious *and* nutritious fare. Rest assured because all were personally visited and screened by myself, a nutritional consultant, and my co-taster, Alex Van Buren, an accomplished New York City food critic.

This book is about helping you make better, more informed choices. In fact, it's my intention that you actually will *crave* healthier food after reading it. You'll learn that there's no one right way to eat for everyone—a theory called bio-individuality. (Makes sense, right? After all, do you use the same shampoo as all of your friends? Why should food be any different?) Sure, there's a lot of nutritional information out there, but talk about confusing. That's why this guide provides an easy-to-follow education about the most important foods you will encounter when dining out. That way, you can use your knowledge to implement the life-changing diet that's right for *you*.

---

3 WAYS YOU CAN USE THIS BOOK

- To find healthy and tasty restaurants in Manhattan.
- To learn how to change your eating habits when you dine out—and in.
- To transform your life by seeing how eating healthier can be pleasurable and startlingly simple.

By now you're probably asking yourself: Who *is* this guy? Why should I listen to anything he says? Well, honestly, I'm not that different from you. I want to be healthy, so I can enjoy my life and contribute to making the world a better place. Rather than bore you with a long report about my life (you can learn more by visiting cleanplatesnyc.com), I'll touch on a few highlights for your peace of mind.

After deferring my acceptance to medical school for a decade-long stint as a successful entrepreneur, I decided that I needed to figure out my health and happiness. As part of that journey, I not only became a certified nutritional consultant, yoga instructor and wellness counselor, but also healed myself from chronic irritable bowel syndrome (IBS), fatigue and skin issues. I'm now a Wellness Counselor backed by seven years of immersing myself in the formal study of nutrition—and four years of working with clients. I've had some amazing teachers: Andrew Weil, M.D., Deepak Chopra and Walter Willett, the head of nutrition at Harvard, in addition to many experts in the fields of Raw Foods, Chinese Medicine, Ayurveda, Macrobiotics, Vegetarianism and High-Protein Diets.

For my clients, and in this book, I synthesize those dietary theories in an easy-to-use format—always keeping an open mind to discovering the truth about what actually works for each individual. Thanks to my experiences, I've had several insights over the years about how we eat, all of which I will be sharing in more detail in *Clean Plates NYC*:

- Eating well is the easiest and best way (along with exercise and perhaps meditation) to positively affect your health and improve your quality of life.
- Contrary to conventional wisdom, healthy eating can be enjoyable and satisfying, free from the typical guilt and confusion we usually feel in relation to eating.
- No single way of eating works for everyone, but there is a healthy way to eat that's just right for *you* and your body.
- A quick way to upgrade your well-being: Select higher-quality versions of whatever foods you're currently consuming, especially when it comes to animal-based products.

- To increase nutrient intake and boost immunity, start with food that's fresh (locally grown), non-toxic (organic) and mostly plant-based (more vegetables, fruits, nuts and seeds). Think of it as a tasty trio—local non-toxic plants.
- Reducing your intake of artificial, chemical-laden processed foods, as well as sugar, caffeine and alcohol, will have you feeling better immediately.
- Making small improvements over time leads to significant change.
- What's good for you is usually good for the environment. Growing food locally means less energy consumption. Organic items don't poison the earth. And a reduction in the demand for livestock frees up vital resources.
- It's entirely possible to commit to values of health and conscious consumerism *and* fully enjoy the pleasures of life and this wonderful city. Why? Because, increasingly, tasty and healthy food is accessible to everyone from vegans to carnivores.

One of the major reasons I wrote this book is there's a real lack of helpful, well-organized information for people who wish to dine out mindfully and still enjoy the experience of eating. Sure, cooking at home is important and many nutrition books offer delicious recipes, but the truth is, we New Yorkers eat out a lot—it is part of the culture. Our city boasts amazing chefs and a stunning variety of cuisines; if you live here, it's likely that restaurants are where you get a huge proportion of your nourishment. During my preliminary investigations, I noted a few gaps in the advice offered by other books and websites: 1) It's easy to find places that list vegan and vegetarian establishments—but none adequately distinguish which spots are healthy (not all are) or which would be appealing for non-vegetarians. 2) Few are dedicated to omnivores who would like to frequent places that serve organic, local and sustainably-raised animal products, and those that do exist tend to be confusing, not comprehensive, not screened for taste and poorly researched. That's why I created *Clean Plates NYC* to be the most exceptionally well-researched, comprehensive and easy-to-use guide that exists; I'm certain it will help you navigate the ever-expanding maze of Manhattan's healthiest and tastiest restaurants.

The main inspiration for this book, however, grew out of my interactions with my clients. Several years ago, I began researching "healthy restaurants" because I believed that I could both eat healthier and enjoy the pleasures and diversity of this wonderful city. As I shared my ever-growing list of healthier restaurants with my clients, they actually started implementing changes and feeling better—a fact that inspired me to thoroughly expand my research, hire an amazing food critic, and set out to create *Clean Plates NYC*. What I learned from counseling clients was that real change calls for practical tools. I think of this book as one of those significant tools.

This project is an extension of the work that I do with my clients, a way to reach more people and contribute to a growing awareness of healthy, responsible and sustainable eating. Together, let's shatter the myth that healthier eating is a sacrifice and prove that we can do it without the guilt, inconvenience, boredom and sheer lack of long-term success that characterize the usual diets.

You see, eating clean food is admirable, but I am equally interested in clean plates—the kind of food that makes you want to lick your dishes.

In good health,

Jared Koch

HOW TO USE THIS BOOK

JUST AS THERE'S NO one-size-fits-all diet for everyone, there's no one right way to read and use this book. But I'd like to point out several helpful features.

Take It With You Everywhere

Constructed to be small and lightweight, *Clean Plates NYC* is easy to slip in a bag or back pocket, and its rounded corners will keep it from getting dog-eared. No matter where you are in Manhattan, you'll be able to quickly locate a restaurant that serves a healthy, delicious version of the cuisine you're in the mood for—from fast food to fine dining, vegan to omnivore and any combination thereof. Don't want to keep it on you? Another option is to store one at home and one at the office (hey, I won't stop you from buying two—the price has been kept low to make the book accessible to as many people as possible).

Learn More About Healthier Eating

Take a peek at the sections of the book preceding the restaurant reviews, where I lay out my *Five Precepts for Eating Well*. In those sections, I also provide an easy-to-follow education on the pros and cons of all the different foods you're likely to encounter at restaurants. From beef to milk to cheese to less-known items like kefir, I've got you covered. Due to the guide's size and scope, it's not a comprehensive list or discussion, but rather a very strong foundation from which you can make intelligent and informed choices. Armed with my *Five Precepts* and a clear understanding of different foods, you'll be able to implement healthier eating habits immediately.

Find the Healthy Restaurant You Want with Easy-to-Use Listings

I don't want anyone to be left out. So whether you're a vegetarian, vegan or meat-eater—and whether you want to spend lavishly or lightly— I've tracked down restaurants for you (always serving delicious meals, naturally). *Clean Plates NYC* boasts an incredibly diverse array of over 200 establishments (including reviews in alphabetical order of our 75 favorites) representing all manner of cuisines, budgets and geographic locations. Among many other options, you'll find (a) the best-tasting hormone and antibiotic-free animal products; (b) the best-tasting high-quality vegetarian dishes; and (c) the best-tasting naturally sweetened desserts.

Get Extra Information From the Glossary, Appendices and Chef Interviews

I believe that clarity leads to better eating, so I've tried to clear up confusion in as many ways as possible. The glossary defines oft-heard, but sometimes-misunderstood terms; the appendices offer a way to quickly reference what you are looking for in a variety of different configurations from geography to top date spots. And as an added bonus the restaurant review section includes interviews with seven of the city's best chefs, who dish about healthy and sustainable foods.

Discover How Eating Well Can Be Fun, Guilt-Free and Life-Changing

I like to think of this book as a tool. It gives you the information you need to eat healthier—with little effort, since the book does the work for you—and puts to rest the excuse that healthy foods are too inaccessible and expensive to incorporate into your life. And then there's the domino effect: When you crave better food and eat more of it, your body responds, rewarding you with better moods, energy and health.

Save the World While You're At It

As a Wellness Counselor, I believe in caring for the world around you— an attitude that can become the impetus for environmentally positive actions like selecting organic, local food.

Register Your Purchase at cleanplatesnyc.com for Extra Benefits

As an owner of *Clean Plates NYC*, you get more than this book. Register your purchase at cleanplatesnyc.com to receive six months free access to our online searchable database of restaurants and also owner privileges such as e-mail updates about new restaurants, restaurant promotions, educational tele-seminars and more.

In addition, you'll get a chance to join our online community and share your thoughts and questions with me and others who are committed to eating healthier foods—but unwilling to forgo the pleasures of eating. To register, use code: imhealthy

RESTAURANT REVIEW PROCESS AND CRITERIA

THIS BOOK IS MEANT to be an indispensable resource for your real-life needs: It's practical, easy to use, easy to follow...and life changing. Yes, life changing. Because if you start eating at several of the 75 restaurants we recommend, I can almost guarantee that you'll feel better, become healthier and begin to crave food that's good for you.

Maybe you're a vegetarian with a meat-eating, foodie spouse. Or a workaholic who orders in takeout at the office. Or an Upper West Side resident. Or perhaps you're all three. No matter what, this book features a restaurant for you. In fact, it has a restaurant for nearly every permutation of taste, cuisine and geographic preference: Upscale and fast food, East Village and East Midtown, Japanese and Italian, vegetarian, vegan, meat-serving and much more.

There are only two constants. Every single featured restaurant serves *delicious* and *nutritious* dishes. How'd we find them? In the next several paragraphs, I explain.

Why We Used a Food Critic and a Nutritionist

Eating healthy foods is considerably more appealing when you enjoy what you're eating—yet most health-food guides give scant attention to taste. Not this one. This one should please the most critical, severe and snobbish of foodies. How can I be sure? Well, after interviewing several seasoned writers, I selected Alex Van Buren, a former *Time Out New York* food writer and *Martha Stewart Living* research editor. We had to agree on every restaurant as far as taste goes; if she or I didn't think it served delicious food, it didn't make it into this book. And as a Wellness Counselor and Nutrition Consultant, I screened and visited every spot to make sure its meals were healthy. How can you be certain you're going to get a healthy *and* delicious meal? Just eat at one of the 75 featured restaurants in *Clean Plates NYC*.

How We Found the Restaurants

My goal was to compile a list of healthy Manhattan restaurants that accommodated both vegetarians and carnivores—and was as wide-ranging as possible. From there, Alex (the food critic) and I would whittle it down to the very best. Already I had a small file of such establishments, assembled over the years; I added to it by tracking down healthy eateries in every way possible. I read other guidebooks, searched online, asked restaurant owners, petitioned my friends and literally walked and drove around the city looking for places. The result: A master list of a couple hundred restaurants. True, I may have missed a few—this is New York City, after all, home to a dizzying array of eateries; plus, before now, there hasn't been a good resource for vegetarians and especially carnivores seeking healthy, but tasty foods. In fact, that's one of the reasons why I also set up a website (cleanplatesnyc.com) where you can stay up-to-date, share your opinions, and give and receive information about closings and openings.

The Screening, Researching, Reviewing and Fact-Checking Process

First, I subjected each place on our master list of several hundred restaurants to a health-screening process. Posing as a potential customer over the phone, I queried the staff about their preparation and sourcing methods (examples: Is your meat hormone- and antibiotic-free? Is it grass-fed? What is your apple pie sweetened with? Do you use a microwave?). In addition, I thoroughly reviewed the menu online or in person.

If the restaurant passed this initial health test, Alex and I visited it incognito (so that we wouldn't receive special treatment). We ordered as wide a variety of foods as possible—appetizers, side dishes, main courses and desserts—and didn't just stick to our own tastes. In addition, we asked the staff more questions, some a repeat of what I'd asked on the phone (more examples: Is your water filtered? Is your produce local and organic?).

Next, Alex and I discussed whether the restaurant met our taste and health criteria; again, we had to agree as far as taste goes. After we selected a restaurant, I or someone on my team called to inform them about their inclusion in this book and to fact-check our details (with an owner, manager or chef) one final time.

Our Criteria

We struggled between being selective and comprehensive and, in the end, decided it was important to offer a hybrid of both. When choosing a restaurant, we took the following areas into consideration:

- Taste
- Atmosphere
- Type of cuisine: We wanted to make sure a wide variety of cuisines were included, from pizza and burgers to Indian and French foods, and on and on. And we added extra points for accessibility, such as when a vegetarian restaurant had a menu that most carnivores would enjoy or when a carnivore-friendly place offered several vegetarian options.
- Lifestyle: To ensure that personal tastes and needs were met, we included casual, power-lunch, fast-food and fine-dining establishments, as well as those that are family-friendly and date-worthy—and more. So if you're, say, a CEO who occasionally craves fast-food, we have you covered (and that's *healthier* fast-food, naturally).
- Geography: Wherever you find yourself in Manhattan—wherever you live, work, shop and hang out—we've identified a restaurant nearby that serves healthy and delicious meals.
- Healthfulness of ingredients: All of our featured restaurants that serve animal products source, at the very minimum, animals raised hormone and antibiotic-free.

In addition, we awarded points for restaurants that:

- Source grass-fed, organic, free-range animals
- Order from small, local farms

- Include a high percentage of vegetables on the menu
- Purchase produce from organic or local purveyors
- Filter their water
- Use high-quality salts
- Offer naturally sweetened desserts
- Include organic and biodynamic wines and organic coffees on their menu
- Sell better-quality soda and soft drinks
- Have wheat- and gluten-free options

We deducted points from restaurants that:
- Offer animal foods that weren't sustainably raised (even if a restaurant sold some sustainably raised meats, we still knocked off points if *every* meat dish didn't fit the bill)
- Use too many fake soy products
- Have too much seitan, a wheat-gluten product used as a fake-meat substitute
- Don't include enough vegetable options or greens on the menu
- Follow poor-quality cooking methods, such as frying
- Cook with poor-quality oils
- Overemphasize dairy, shellfish, veal and foie gras

Our 75 Featured Selections: Clean Plates Approved!

In alphabetical order, the 75 best restaurants—the places that passed our taste and health tests with very high scores—are given informative and entertaining reviews by Alex. For easier browsing, we include icons that provide key information (Is it vegetarian? Does it serve animal foods? Is it a good budget pick?).

If you simply stick to eating at a combination of these 75 restaurants when you dine out, there's a good chance that you'll improve your quality of life and your health. Why? Well, for one thing, you'll be putting better foods into your body, and it will respond in kind. For another, you'll start to associate delicious meals with healthy meals—

and you'll begin to crave the latter. In fact, consuming junk food will seem less and less appealing. And you'll be doing all of this with little effort because the restaurant—and this book—have done the work for you. All you have to do is eat!

Honorable Mentions

As well as the 75 winners, we're including what I like to call The Runners-Up: Restaurants that didn't quite live up to all of our criteria. One of these supplemental lists is of eateries that passed our health tests, but not our taste test; we visited all of these places. The other is of establishments that didn't pass our health tests; in some cases, we visited them and they served delicious food, but just weren't healthy enough. In other cases, we didn't visit the restaurant because it didn't get past our initial screening, but we're including it in the supplemental list because it's doing a decent job using sustainable ingredients.

Nevertheless, most of our honorable mentions are better for you than any old restaurant. If you go to one of these eateries, ask questions and be discerning—and you're likely to eat a delicious and healthy meal.

In addition, the review section includes my 15 favorite Manhattan health-food markets, all spots where you can purchase healthy prepared foods. Often these markets are good options for quick meals; in the review section, I've indicated which ones have seating.

Again, we'd love to hear about places you think we missed and get your comments about the restaurants we've chosen; maybe you think a few of the benchwarmers should have made the featured list or some on our featured list don't deserve to be there. So be sure to register your purchase at cleanplatesnyc.com, where you'll join a community of like-minded people interested in eating healthier and more responsibly but still with great pleasure.

WHY EAT HEALTHIER?

For Physical Health and Quality of Life

FINANCIAL COLUMNISTS LIKE TO point out that ordering a $3 latte every day adds up to $1,000 a year that otherwise would have been accruing interest in a CD. Our daily food choices operate according to similar principles; instead of building up our financial assets, however, we are building our health resources.

Several cases in point: You wake up, yawning, get dressed, and (a) start the day with a cup of herbal tea or glass of water with lemon to accompany your bowl of oatmeal and fruit; or (b) pick up a Starbucks coffee with sugar on your way to work, skipping breakfast. Later the same day, you and your co-workers order out for (a) wild salmon with vegetables and brown rice; or (b) fast-food hamburgers and fries. You get the picture: Going for the "b" option day in and day out adds up to nothing good, while a lifetime of "a" choices equals a lifetime of overall optimal well-being.

That's why we should remind ourselves why it's worth it to be healthy (um, better looks, lower weight!). But, actually, how about: more energy, feeling better, lower healthcare bills, better sex. So think about those benefits—good sex, more energy, better moods—the next time you're tempted by the often-insidious forces that affect our food choices, like instant gratification, biochemical addiction, emotional and peer pressure, and just plain old habit.

Our health may be affected more by the foods we eat than by any other factor. I think that's great news, since it means we can do something about it. Of course, exercise, sleep and genetics—not to mention our relationships, career and spirituality—count, too. But the reason "you are what you eat" has endured as a phrase is because what we consume builds, fuels, cleanses or—unfortunately—pollutes our very cells.

At the end of the day, it all comes down to choices.

For the World Beyond Your Plate

Here's a new one: An organic apple a day keeps the greenhouse gases away. Translation? Eating naturally is good for nature. It's not only physical health that inspires me to be conscious about what I eat—it's also the environment. Here's a list of simple ways to positively affect the planet through your food choices.

1. CUT DOWN ON ANIMAL PRODUCTS.

No need to go vegetarian to reduce your impact. But consuming less meat—poultry, beef, fish, dairy and eggs—is a powerful way to help the earth. I hope the following facts motivate you to skip a main course of meat or dine at a vegetarian restaurant now and then, even if you're an omnivore.

- Wasted water. Beef is one of the worst offenders; its production in the United States alone requires more water than growing the world's fruit and vegetable crop.
- Wasted land. Livestock consume grain that uses up many acres.
- Wasted energy. It takes ten times more fossil fuel to produce a meat-based diet than a plant-based one. That statistic led the United Nations to declare "Raising animals for food generates more greenhouse gases than all the cars and trucks in the world combined."

• Wasteful, er, waste. Don't picture this while you're eating, but imagine the amount of sewage generated by farm animals, which comprise three times the number of humans on the planet.

2. STOCK UP ON ORGANIC FOODS.

More toxic than ever before, pesticides and herbicides contaminate the soil, water and air, which in turn poison both humans and wildlife. So support restaurants that source organic products or suggest that your favorite local eatery consider purchasing from Certified Naturally Grown Farms (certifiednaturallygrown.org), an organization that exceeds USDA organic standards and is locally based in upstate New York.

3. GO YIMBY (YES IN MY BACKYARD) BY CHOOSING LOCALLY GROWN FOODS.

Most food travels from the farm to the restaurant on a long-distance trek, gobbling up fuel and requiring environmentally damaging packaging. As Stephen Hopp says in his wife Barbara Kingsolver's book *Animal, Vegetable, Miracle*, "If every U.S. citizen ate just one meal a week composed of locally and organically raised meats and produce, we would reduce our country's oil consumption by over 1.1 million barrels of oil every week."

> **TIP: A WORD OF CAUTION**
>
> Just because locally grown and organic foods are better for the environment doesn't mean they're always healthier for our bodies. Locally grown organic sugar? Sorry, still sugar to your body.

4. AVOID GMOS.

The name certainly doesn't sound healthy: Genetically modified organisms, aka GMOs. These artificially altered crops require an enormous amount of pesticides (they even produce pesticides within their own cells), and they cross-contaminate other crops and harm wildlife. The majority of soy (as in tofu), corn and wheat crops are now GMO plants; if these items are staples in your diet, frequent eateries that serve organic versions.

5. SAYONARA TO BOTTLED WATER.

Americans use two million plastic bottles *every five minutes*. Imagine them all stacked up in a pile. The amount of oil needed to make those bottles equals about 15 million barrels a year. Even recycling them means using more fossil fuels. Opt for filtered water when available and encourage restaurant owners to invest in a filtration system.

WHAT'S MORE IMPORTANT: LOCALLY GROWN OR ORGANIC?

Organic but non-local produce is free of pesticides harmful to our bodies and the soil but requires extra energy to travel from farm to table and loses nutrients along the way. *Locally Grown* but non-organic goods retain most of their nutrients because of the speed at which they get to our plates, but they may be sprayed with chemicals, which are damaging to our bodies, the soil and the atmosphere. *The answer:* Unfortunately, if you can't get an item locally grown and organic, there is no easy answer. It is a matter of personal choice and if you choose one or the other you are doing pretty good.

DESIGN YOUR OWN DIET

I BELIEVE THERE *IS* a dream diet for everyone—it's just not the same for each person. That brings me to a key principle of this book:

THE FIRST PRECEPT:
There's no one right way to eat for everyone.

As nutrition pioneer Roger Williams writes in his groundbreaking 1950s book *Biochemical Individuality*, "If we continue to try to solve problems on the basis of the average man, we will be continually in a muddle. Such a man does not exist."

We're all biochemically—genetically, hormonally and so on—different, and the idea that this should guide our eating habits has recently begun to excite the leading-edge medical and nutrition community. Experts are beginning to talk about the benefits of individualizing our diets rather than giving advice based on recommended daily allowances (RDA) or the United States Department of Agriculture's (USDA's) food pyramid, both created with the "average" person in mind.

How We Differ

As you read through my list of how we're all unique, some of the points may seem obvious (of course someone training for a marathon requires different foods than someone sitting in front of a computer all day, for instance). But part of what I'd like to get across is that these distinctions manifest themselves not only between individuals, but also between your different selves—your tired self, your active self and the like. The key is to pay attention to how your body reacts to various foods and to what it's telling you at any given moment.

- Genetic Makeup: To a large extent, the anatomy and body chemistry that you inherited from your ancestors determine your nutritional needs and ability to benefit from particular foods. For example, a few recent studies have shown that some people possess the genetic ability to metabolize caffeine more efficiently than others. Research has also revealed that specific groups of people have the genetic makeup to absorb vitamin B12 with ease, or benefit greatly from broccoli's cancer-fighting nutrients—while others lack those genes.

- Culture and Background: Your ethnicity and upbringing influence how your body acts. For instance, several of my friends have inherited a genetic ability enabling them to drink milk, but my friend who is Asian is lactose intolerant, as are many of his compatriots—his grandparents came to America from a country where milk rarely makes it onto the menu. So it's helpful to consider which foods are part of your culture and background, and incorporate the appropriate ones into your diet.

- Lifestyle: A man training for a marathon requires different foods than a person who does an hour of yoga each week.

- Day-to-day physical health: Pay attention to your physical-health symptoms to figure out what foods you need. Sick? Miso soup may be just the thing. Sneezing constantly? Avoid dairy and sugar; the former causes the body to produce mucus and the latter weakens the immune system.

- Gender: Whether you're a man or a woman affects your diet needs. For example, menstruating women require more iron than men, but men need more zinc than their female counterparts to nourish their reproductive systems.

- Age: A growing, active teen will be ravenous at dinnertime; the same person, 60 years later, will likely find that his appetite is waning.

- Seasons and Climate: Even the weather affects what's best for you to eat. When it's hot outside, the body will likely crave cooling foods like salads; on a cold winter day, hot soup is probable.

Eating as a Bio-Individual

The philosophy that no single way of eating is right for everyone isn't new. Both Traditional Chinese Medicine and India's Ayurvedic system revolve around prescribing the most appropriate diet for specific categories of body types and constitutions.

More recent incarnations of these ancient approaches include the blood-type diet and metabolic typing. The blood-type diet was made famous a decade ago by naturopath Peter D'Adamo, who theorized (to put it very simply) that people with blood type O do best eating meat, but type A's thrive as vegetarians. The thinking behind the discovery? Type O's descended from ancient hunters while type A's came from agricultural civilizations. The idea behind metabolic typing (again, to put it simply) is that your metabolism dictates the appropriate percentage of proteins or carbohydrates in your diet; those who metabolize proteins well require extra animal foods, while others do better with more carbs.

Not everyone agrees. Proponents of *The China Study*, a 2005 book by two nutritional biochemists who conducted a 20-year survey of Chinese diets, argue that animal consumption is the leading cause of human disease, while followers of Weston A. Price, a dentist who carried out extensive health research in many countries, rely on culturally based studies to back up their claim that animal proteins and organ meats have benefits. Ultimately, the jury is still out (and probably always will be) on whether we have evolved to be omnivores or vegetarians. Though I do believe in the importance of our culture moving more toward a vegetarian-based diet, I have also observed that, while some people thrive on a vegetarian or vegan diet, others do not—some people require (high-quality) animal protein to function optimally.

HOW SHOULD YOU APPROACH OTHER DIETARY THEORIES?

One diet (it's pushing it to call it a dietary theory!) that most of us would like to move away from is the standard American diet (or SAD, as I call it). So what should we move toward? Well, we all have different needs, but that doesn't mean we have to invent diets from scratch. We have help: Other established dietary theories. It's worth knowing about them, so you can consider which parts of each work for you.

For instance, if you're energetic, enjoy a challenge and possess a strong digestive system, you fit the description of a good candidate for raw foodism. It's a relatively new diet based on ancient principles in which vegetables, fruits, nuts and seeds are served uncooked—or heated to a maximum of 118 degrees Fahrenheit in order to maintain nutrients and enzymes. Fit the description but balking at consuming only uncooked foods? Maybe partial raw foodism is right for you (say, 50 percent raw and 50 percent cooked). Or perhaps you're eager to transition away from junk food or dairy and are very disciplined and love Asian food to boot; in that case, a macrobiotic diet may be right for you. It's a route that heavily emphasizes rice, however, so it's not the best choice for someone who doesn't do well on grains. And for many people, considering vegetarianism makes sense. If you do decide to experiment with not eating meat, be sure to avoid the pitfalls that many vegans and vegetarians accidentally step into—namely, eating too many processed foods, carbohydrates, dairy and sugar, as well as consuming too much soy in the form of fake-meat products.

Still confused? Think of it as designing your own diet using bits and pieces of good, but different, ideas. The point is that you don't need to adhere to any particular theory (they all have their pros and cons and none are right for everyone). Instead, tailor what you eat to your biology, body, blood type, hormones, tastes and way of looking at the world. My next four precepts will help to guide your choices.

How We're the Same

Our food choices often become another way of separating us. Especially when there are moral underpinnings to our choices, it's tempting to think that "my way is the only right way to eat." What I like most about bio-individuality is that the focus is on how our physical selves can achieve their fullest potential. In my opinion, when that happens— when we're able to thrive physically—then we've created an unshakeable foundation for living to our fullest potential and for making a meaningful contribution to our collective well-being as a species and a planet.

Being different should bring us together. Why? Well, partially because it's about realizing that other people have needs distinct from ours. Some types love to begin their day with a shot of wheatgrass—but perhaps the thought makes you turn green. And while your friends can't imagine living without an occasional hamburger or slice of pizza, maybe you thrive on hearty salads and raw foods. And we all know that irritating person who can gobble up everything in sight and remain slim—a profile that many of us don't have. Hopefully being aware of these distinctions will lead us to be less critical of others—and less likely to feel guilty about our own choices. Judgment and guilt, after all, are bad for your health. At the very least, they really mess with your digestion.

BIO-INDIVIDUALITY MEANS THAT THERE'S no perfect diet for everyone. There *is*, however, the perfect food for everyone—real food. It's what we're designed to eat, regardless of our lifestyle, genetic makeup and other differences. Which leads me to my next premise.

THE SECOND PRECEPT: The overwhelming majority of your diet should consist of natural, high-quality and whole foods.

Which means...what? What, exactly, is real food? It's a question I often get from my clients. Once upon a time, it had an obvious answer, but, over the past hundred years, food has become increasingly unlike itself: Processed, altered with chemicals, dyed unnatural colors, flavored with suspect ingredients and generally turned as artificial as can be.

These kinds of changes generally result in more toxins and fewer nutrients. In my opinion, the success of diets like macrobiotics and raw foods in claiming to help heal diabetes and even cancer (according to some studies) is due in large part to the fact that both diets call for increasing your intake of real, high quality, whole foods while reducing consumption of artificial and chemical-laden dishes.

TIP: DON'T GET SIDETRACKED BY FOCUSING ONLY ON CALORIES

Many people equate reducing calories with a healthier lifestyle, but I firmly believe that the quality of the foods we eat are much more important—even when it comes to losing weight. Here's a way of looking at it: Think of food as fuel. Does a car run best on poor-quality fuel? No, of course not. And our bodies are the same: They need optimal fuel. Another way of looking at it is to ask yourself: What's better for my body—1,800 calories of junk food and candy bars, or 2,000 calories of vegetables and fruits? I think you get the idea!

All this means we desperately need to get back to basics. To help you with the terms (high quality, whole, natural) and to give you an answer to the question above (What, exactly, is real food?), read on.

Real, aka Natural

In this book, I use the terms *real* and *natural* synonymously, a fact that may help you distinguish real from artificial. Knowing what's natural is largely a matter of intuition and common sense; it's not as if you're going to start bringing a checklist to restaurants.

Nevertheless, you'll become a pro at identifying the real thing more quickly if you ask yourself a couple of questions the next time you eat. These questions include: What would I eat if I lived in the wild? What has the earth and nature provided for humans to eat? What have I, as a human, evolved to eat? To keep it simple, focus on what grows out of the ground or on a tree. In addition, think vegetables, fruits, nuts, seeds, beans, grains, herbs and animal foods.

TIP: AN EASY WAY TO FIGURE OUT IF IT'S REAL FOOD

Just ask yourself this question: Was it made in nature or in a factory? Visualize where the item began its life. Perhaps you'll see it hanging on a bush, growing on a tree, sprouting up from the earth or grazing in a field. If it's fizzing to life in a test tube, move on.

Quality

A peach from the grocery store is a real-food item—it was made in nature and wasn't flavored in a factory—but that doesn't mean it's the best quality. The more of the following qualities the peach has, the higher its quality: it's organic, with fewer chemicals and more nutrients than its non-organic counterpart; locally grown, so it requires less artificial ripening and storage, and loses fewer nutrients en route from farm to plate; non-irradiated, since radiation destroys nutrients and changes an item's chemical structure; and not genetically modified (non-GMO), an unnatural process with unknown consequences.

In addition, ask yourself if additives, flavorings, coloring or preservatives were used. It's not always obvious in a restaurant, but it's worth considering. For instance, a cupcake with fire-engine red icing probably has, among other things, icing that's artificially colored.

Whole

This term is about processes and cooking methods: The fewer things done to a food, the better. Basically, cooking and preparing food makes it less whole — but that doesn't necessarily mean the dish in question is unhealthy.

Raw foods (that is, uncooked) are in their natural state with their nutrients intact. Yet cooking is often considered the first step in the digestive process. Why? Well, it breaks down the food's cell walls and fiber, making it easier to absorb the food's nutrients. Although I am not typically a proponent of a 100% Raw-Food diet, I do believe that we should aim to eat a significant amount of raw foods as well as some cooked foods. The ratio will ultimately depend on the strength of your digestive system and personal tastes.

When examining the healthfulness of a prepared dish, you should consider:

- The cooking methods used. Err on the side of undercooking, since prolonged exposure to high heat destroys nutrients, enzymes and water content. Examples: Steaming or poaching (good) versus frying (not good) or microwaving (bad).
- The wholeness of the ingredients. Examples: A bowl of berries (good) versus fruit juice with sugar (not good).
- The number of steps or processes used to make the food. Examples: A bowl of oatmeal made from whole oats (good) versus cereal made into flakes (not so good).

What to Ask

Some establishments make meals from scratch, while others pre-make recipes in bulk and microwave them on demand. To find out whether your dish is real, quality and whole, ask the staff to confirm your meal's origins, ingredients and preparation techniques.

The kinds of questions you might have include whether brown rice can be substituted for white; if the cheese is raw or pasteurized; if the cakes are made with butter (real) or margarine (fake); whether the salmon is artificially colored or is the genuine wild-harvested article; and if the beef comes from a grass-fed cow or one fattened with grains, antibiotics and growth hormones.

I also like to know if the vegetables on my plate have just been steamed or whether the only kitchen tool required was a can opener. Peas from a can, for instance, often come with added salt. The same goes for fruit. Say there's a restaurant that lists peaches and cream on the dessert menu. Are those high-quality, real peaches, or the kind that come out of a can where they've been marinating in flavored-sugar syrup?

A Word About Beverages

And don't forget the drinks. Is the water filtered or from the city's chlorinated supply? The former is actually closer to fresh, natural water. Is the soda sweetened with fruit juice or with high-fructose corn syrup? And that coffee—decaffeinated naturally?

Think of these ideas as practice exercises for your "food radar"—a muscle of sorts that will grow stronger with use. The more you check for the differences between whole and unwholesome, high quality and run-of-the-mill, real and processed, the more automatic eating real, whole and high-quality foods will become.

Foods For Thought

Fats, sweeteners, grains, animal products: They sound like basics, but they come in many guises—and are the cause of many debates. Take bread. Mom always told you it was an essential source of fiber, but your newspaper's science section just ran an article about how humans aren't designed to eat grains. At any rate, you're not going to forswear bread completely because you love it—but should you pair it with butter or with margarine? The latter, after all, contains fewer calories. But wasn't there a television report the other day about the evils of margarine?

The fact is, confusion and controversy surround many types of food—some more than others. To clear things up and to give you the tools to design your own diet, I've compiled information about various foods and food categories, from vegetables and fruits to meat and dairy. What you learn will enable you to make smart dietary choices.

WHAT I'M ABOUT TO say might be difficult to absorb—not because you've never heard it before, but rather because you've heard it, in some form, thousands of times. But let me tell you what it is, and then I'll address figuring out how to make it stick:

THE THIRD PRECEPT:

Everyone would be better off if a larger proportion of their diet consisted of plants—mostly vegetables (in particular, leafy greens), along with some nuts, seeds and fruits.

To get this message to sink in, I encourage clients to think about it in big, overarching terms. I like to point out that eating plants is a way of taking in the energy of the sun. As a life force, the sun contributes to our health and sense of well-being enormously. Without it there would be no life on earth. Want more of it? Eat more plants. They're a more direct source of "sun food" than meat; when we eat animals, we are indirectly consuming what they themselves already ate.

If this concept is a bit too esoteric, consider it from a scientific point of view. What gives green plants their color? It's chlorophyll, the pigment in leaves that enables them to absorb the sun's rays using a process called photosynthesis. Many nutritionists believe that when we eat green leaves, we take in that stored solar energy. Chlorophyll enriches blood, kills germs, detoxifies the bloodstream and liver, reduces bodily odors and controls the appetite.

Still snoozing off when you hear "eat more plants"? Maybe telling yourself "get more sun food" will provide the necessary motivation instead.

To help you navigate between different types of plants, the following two sections of this book are devoted to information about vegetables and fruits. It's not wrong to eat meat—in fact, it can be healthy for certain people—but eat lots of plants, and you'll start to feel better. The next two sections show you why.

THINK ABOUT IT: YET ANOTHER REASON TO EAT VEGGIES

Have you ever heard of anyone being overweight or getting heart disease or cancer from eating too many vegetables?

Veggie Tales

Pity the unappreciated vegetable. Perpetually shunted to the side—as a garnish, appetizer, side dish—it rarely gets to give all that it has to offer. What does it offer, you ask? An enormous amount of nutrients and health-boosting properties in the form of vitamins, minerals, fiber, phytochemicals and antioxidants. Vegetables should form the bulk of your diet

---

QUICK DEFINITION: ANTIOXIDANTS

Their name says it all: They're *anti*-oxidants. They counteract oxidation—and the free radicals believed to speed up aging and disease. A variety of elements cause our bodies to produce excess free radicals. Some are "bad," like toxic air and the chemicals to which we're exposed, but some are everyday, such as exercise and the normal process of metabolizing food for energy. Fortunately, you can combat these excess free radicals by eating more vegetables (as well as fruits, nuts and seeds), which are abundant in antioxidants.

If you're a vegetarian, aim to increase the proportion of veggies that you consume relative to the amount of grains, beans, dairy, sugar and tofu in your diet. Similarly, omnivores should be mindful of the meat-to-vegetable ratio in each meal.

And I'd like to take a moment to remind you about my second premise—eat high-quality, natural and whole vegetables. For one thing, they taste noticeably better. In addition, local, organic vegetables suffer less nutrient loss than their long-distance counterparts; they also reap the benefits of organic soils, which are rich in nutrients.

In addition, these do-it-all veggies possess a characteristic that many people don't know to look for but that's important for good health: They're alkalizing. In contrast, most foods in the standard American diet—especially meats, sugar and white flour—are acid-forming. Without getting into the nitty-gritty science of it, I'd like to point out that most disease states within the body occur in an acidic environment. Foods that create alkalinity are healthier.

To help you order at restaurants, here's a roundup of the types of vegetables you're likely to encounter—and how they affect your body:

QUICK TIP: SQUEEZE SOME LEMON IN YOUR WATER

A one-question quiz: Is a lemon acidic or alkalizing for the body? Well, even though lemons taste acidic, they're actually one of the most alkalizing foods as far as the chemistry they produce in your blood.

LEAFY GREENS should be a priority because they're one of the most nutrient-dense foods. Chock-full of chlorophyll, they also boast a calcium-to-magnesium ratio that makes them great bone builders and encourages relaxation and appropriate nerve-and-muscle responsiveness, ensuring the body's smooth functioning. And as well as being a good way to obtain iron, vitamin C and folic acid, leafy greens contain essential amino acids, meaning they're an excellent source of protein—one that potentially rivals the kind from animals. Let's take a look at some of the more common leafy greens.

Kale, swiss chard, collards and spinach are all chef favorites. If possible, ask for yours to be lightly steamed or even served raw, both options that retain more nutrients than frying. A quick sauté with garlic is another delicious and healthy alternative.

Spinach enjoys an impressive reputation (think Popeye) but contains oxalic acid, an anti-nutrient that prevents the absorption and use of calcium and may contribute to kidney stones and gout. While some nutritional experts insist that thorough cooking neutralizes the acid, others report that overcooking makes it toxic (the latter group suggest eating it raw). Until there's a definitive answer, I recommend enjoying spinach without overdoing it, and opting instead for kale, swiss chard or collard greens when possible.

Lettuce, mesclun greens, watercress and arugula often appear in salads, meaning they're raw and still contain all their nutrients and enzymes (watercress in particular is rich in B vitamins). But skip iceberg lettuce. The most common salad green in the United States, iceberg lettuce has few nutrients and tends to be heavily sprayed.

Parsley and dandelion greens, both highly nutritious, don't make it onto menus as often as other greens; when they do, it's usually as a garnish or as part of a salad. Parsley is incredibly rich in iron and

TIP: THE INSTA-
NUTRIENT SHOT

Drinking the juice of
any type of green—not
just wheatgrass—is
a speedy way to get
a nutrient infusion
without your teeth or
digestive system having
to work at breaking
down the plants' cell
walls. (Nevertheless,
don't stop eating whole
greens, since they
provide fiber as well as
some nutrients that may
be lost or oxidized in
the juicing process.)

vitamin C, while bitter dandelion—an acquired taste—
offers some vitamin D and helps to cleanse the liver.

Wheatgrass tends to conjure up images of earthy-
crunchy types, but I think a better way to look at it is as
a treat for health connoisseurs. It boasts one of the most
concentrated sources of chlorophyll, a pigment (as you
may recall from earlier) that captures the sun's energy
and passes its healthful effects along to your body. New
Yorkers knock it back like a shot of espresso at juice bars
and health-food restaurants all over the city.

CRUCIFEROUS VEGETABLES are plants in the cabbage
family, a category that includes broccoli, cauliflower,
Brussels sprouts, kale, bok choy and all cabbages (yep,
there's some overlap with the "leafy greens" group).
High in vitamin C and soluble fiber, these foods also are
crammed with nutrients boasting potent anti-cancer
properties. And only cruciferous vegetables contain isothiocyanates, a
nutrient that has been associated with a decrease in lung cancer.

These veggies crop up in all guises on menus, most often as a side (of
broccoli or cauliflower, for instance), but sometimes in stir-fries and
casseroles. And they're common at Asian and raw-food eateries, where
items like broccoli or kale tend to be served raw and marinated—a
preparation method that imparts a sautéed texture without the
nutrient loss that comes with actual sautéing.

ROOT VEGETABLES include carrots, beets, potatoes, parsnips, yams,
turnips and radishes, each with a unique nutritional profile. Carrots,
for instance, contain the antioxidant known as betacarotene; beets,
crammed with iron, enrich the blood. White potatoes, however, have
more sugar and fewer nutrients than yams or sweet potatoes. When
possible, inquire about substituting one of the latter two in potato-
based dishes.

MUSHROOMS probably generate the most controversy of all vegetables, at least as far as their health claims go. Some nutritionists advise steering clear because they are, after all, fungus, and are therefore potentially infectious. They're also hard to digest. Other experts, however, particularly those who study Asian cultures, vaunt the medicinal properties of mushrooms. Personally, I like to stick to the shiitake and maitake (hen of the woods) varieties, both of which have cancer-fighting and immune-boosting properties (recent studies have suggested that button mushrooms contain several goodies, such as antioxidants, too).

KIMCHI and **SAUERKRAUT** come in what is possibly the best form in which to consume your veggies —raw and fermented. Literally "alive," they teem with nutrients, enzymes and probiotics, which aid digestion.

As central to Korean culture as pasta is to Italy, kimchi may contain any type of vegetable but often includes cabbage and carrots, which are typically spiced up with garlic, ginger or cayenne. Because of its spiciness, kimchi makes not only a great snack, but also a delicious condiment. A German staple, sauerkraut is made from cultured cabbage. Both naturally fermented treats are becoming popular in all types of restaurants as a side dish, in sandwiches or as part of a main course.

QUICK DEFINITION: GOOD GERMS AND ENZYMES

We hear it constantly: Such-and-such food boasts enzymes and probiotics. But what do those funny-sounding things do?

Enzymes control the rate of every chemical reaction in your system, which means that you need them to digest food. So what happens when we don't get our enzymes, which are potentially destroyed by overcooking? Bad digestion. *Probiotics* are healthy bacteria in the gut that rid your intestines of bad stuff. The upshot? You're healthier when you get probiotics.

SEAWEEDS, which I like to think of as vegetables from the sea, include nori (used to wrap sushi), hijiki, wakame, dulse and many others. Extremely dense in minerals, they add a salty, oceanlike taste to dishes.

Asian establishments (in particular Japanese restaurants, as you can probably tell from the aforementioned names) serve seaweed often. So do vegetarian eateries. Not familiar with this food? Try a seaweed salad or ask for extra in your miso soup; both are easy, delicious ways to familiarize yourself with sea veggies—and to enjoy a big, healthy dose of minerals.

Feeling Fruity

Think of them as sweets that are good to eat: Fruits are good sources of fiber, antioxidants, phytochemicals and vitamins, and provide energy via their easily digestible sugars.

They should comprise a small percentage of your overall plant intake, so it's appropriate that fruits make up a small percentage of the amount of plant food offered at restaurants—vegetables pop up all over menus, but fruits tend to appear only in juices, smoothies or desserts.

And don't be concerned about creating huge spikes in blood sugar; it's generally not an issue because fruits come packaged with fiber and other co-factors. (However, people with diabetes or who are prone to candida or yeast infections should go easy on sugary fruits like bananas or grapes, or avoid fruits altogether until their health problem is resolved.) Here are details about fruits you're likely to find on Manhattan menus:

> **QUICK DEFINITION: CO-FACTOR**
>
> A co-factor is a nutrient that helps *another* nutrient work better.

NON-SWEET FRUITS, such as peppers, tomatoes, and cucumbers, rank low on the glycemic index and therefore barely disrupt our blood-sugar balance. People with candida or diabetes can eat them safely. During the summer, I recommend checking out the many delicious varieties of locally grown heirloom tomatoes on offer.

FATTY FRUITS, such as avocadoes and olives, are arguably the best source of fats you can eat, because they are whole and come from plants (in contrast to many processed oils). Eaten raw, as they always should be, avocadoes and olives contain a fat-digesting enzyme, lipase, that makes them easy for our bodies to process. As a bonus, they're an excellent source of protein.

BERRIES are my favorite sweet fruits, both from a culinary perspective and nutritionally speaking. On the glycemic index, they rank lowest of all the sweet fruits, and, individually, each berry is touted for a specific attribute. For instance, blueberries offer a significant number of antioxidants, while raspberries help to nourish the female reproductive system.

In addition, several berries—especially goji berries and açai, the former a tart, bitter Tibetan berry, the latter the fruit of Amazonian palm trees—constitute a relatively new category of foods called superfruits, known as being exceptionally rich in nutrients. Sold in raw-food restaurants, goji berries in particular are also increasingly appearing in health-conscious eateries.

CITRUS FRUITS include oranges, lemons, limes, and grapefruits. They tend to be high in immune-boosting vitamin C and in bioflavonoids—a type of antioxidant known for its anti-cancer properties, as well as its role in keeping blood capillaries healthy. Although citrus fruits taste acidic, they are, in fact, alkalizing and help to counteract the acidity of the meat, grains and beans that typically form the bulk of a restaurant meal.

ORCHARD FRUITS include apples, pears and peaches. Best eaten raw for their enzymes, soluble fiber and nutrients, these fruits usually show up in fruit salads and smoothies.

TROPICAL FRUITS like papayas, mangoes and pineapples are especially rich in the kinds of enzymes that are not only powerful aids to digestion, but also may help to break down scar tissue and waste materials in the body. Of course, being tropical, they're not local to New

York City. Nevertheless, they offer a tasty alternative to refined sugar for someone craving a sweet snack.

Grains and Bread

In many people's minds, grains—a fresh-baked loaf of bread, pasta with tomatoes and garlic—are a bit of an indulgence, okay when eaten here or there, but not to be devoured constantly. And, actually, I agree. If you tolerate them well, grains can add fiber, protein, other nutrients and enjoyment to your diet, as long as they're properly prepared, eaten in moderation, mostly in their whole form (I'll explain shortly) and organic (many grains are heavily sprayed and genetically modified).

That's not to say there aren't drawbacks. In fact, I specifically advise my clients to avoid the complimentary bread basket served before most meals. Why? The body treats grains—especially in the form of flour—like sugar, upsetting your blood-sugar balance and contributing to weight gain and insulin resistance. In addition, unless grains are soaked or sprouted, their bran layer will contain phytic acid, which reduces mineral absorption and enzyme inhibitors, which interfere with digestion. And, overall, grains cause the body to form mucus and are acidic; this last point means that the positive, alkaline effects of eating vegetables are partially neutralized when you eat grains.

So what is the best way to eat grains? Before I answer that, I should emphasize that not all grains are created equal, whether whole or refined. To address those differences, below I discuss the pros and cons of different grains. Overall, however, I recommend eating grains in their intact state (as opposed to milled grains like flour), such as brown rice, barley, oats, quinoa and—best of all—sprouted grains, made by soaking the grain in water until it germinates. Foods that aren't intact include those made from flour like breads, cakes and pasta as well as white rice. (Brown rice is whole, but pasta made from brown-rice flour isn't—although it's preferable to wheat pasta.)

> **QUICK DEFINITION: REFINED GRAINS**
>
> Refined grains are made by removing the bran (the outer layer) and the germ, which is rich in vitamin E. In the removal process, the fiber and most of the nutrients are lost. This is why brown rice is preferable to white. In addition, grains are further refined when they're milled into flour for breads and pasta.

A host of reasons underpin these recommendations. Flour is prone to rancidity. It causes a big, unhealthy spike in blood sugar (because the fiber, which has been removed, isn't there to slow down the release of carbs, which upset the body's blood-sugar balance when they're released too quickly). And refined grains like white rice and bread contain plenty of calories but little nutrition.

White wheat flour is one of the worst of the refined grains. In addition to having few nutrients and containing gluten, it's usually adulterated with bleaching agents and other chemicals to enhance its performance. Unfortunately, it's used in a whopping 90 percent of baked goods. Fortunately, there are some alternatives in addition to the whole grains just discussed.

Preparation techniques make a big difference; traditional methods yield more nutritious, easier-to-digest dishes. For example, the healthiest kind of bread you can order is the aforementioned sprouted grain bread, made from presoaked grains that are baked at low temperatures. Health-food restaurants often offer them. Sourdough bread is another smart choice, since it's naturally leavened with a traditional fermentation technique that neutralizes its phytic acid, increases its nutrients' availability and creates lactobacillus—friendly gut bacteria that aid digestion. And give dosas—a fermented, regional Indian grain product—a try. Made from rice and lentils that have been fermented for at least two days, dosas have a wonderful cheesy taste. Think of them as the south Indian equivalent of burritos—but more nutritious and easier to digest. My favorite choice for breads made directly from flour is spelt and whole rye.

> **TIP: AL DENTE PASTA**
>
> Al dente is the best option for cooked pasta because it only mildly affects your blood-sugar balance; overcooked pasta causes a rapid spike in blood sugar.

Which brings me to a summary of my overall recommendations: Say yes to moderation, traditional preparation methods and whole grains—and no to refined, milled and non-organic versions. An overview of a selection of key grains follows. Although they all contain traces of gluten, I have divided them into gluten grains and non-gluten grains for people who are allergic. Even if you aren't, cutting down on gluten is good for your health.

GLUTEN GRAINS

WHEAT is the highest in gluten of all the grains, which is why it's the
universal choice for bread making—gluten helps bread to rise. It's also
the main ingredient in most pasta, pizza crusts, pastries, crackers,
cakes, cookies and is even used as a thickener in sauces.

The majority of wheat crops are genetically modified (choose
organic!). Given its ubiquity, wheat is not easy to avoid. That, plus the
fact that it has addictive qualities, means that we tend to consume
way too much of it. Nevertheless, I suggest making an effort to steer
clear—or at least cut down—in part because wheat's high gluten level
means it frequently disrupts the digestive system, even if you're not
allergic. Reduce the percentage of wheat in your diet, and I suspect
you'll be pleasantly surprised at how much better you feel day to day.
(Incidentally, Seitan—a popular meat substitute for vegetarians and
vegans—is essentially wheat gluten with the texture of meat, so I
recommend going easy on it.)

BULGUR AND COUSCOUS are actually wheat—tiny cracked pieces of
it—and not a type of grain in their own right. Used like rice, bulgur is
a staple in Middle Eastern restaurants and is best known as the main
ingredient in tabbouleh. Couscous is typically found in North African
or Moroccan cuisine.

KAMUT AND SPELT are non-hybridized, more ancient varieties
of wheat. Because they're lower in gluten than wheat—and more

nutritious to boot—both make good substitutes. In fact, you may do well on spelt even if you're sensitive to gluten, because the grain contains a different form of it. Fortunately, it's fairly easy to find spelt at health-conscious restaurants, where it's becoming increasingly popular as an ingredient for breads, baked goods and pizza crusts.

RYE, rich in a variety of nutrients, is used in place of wheat in items like rye bread and German pumpernickel. People who are mildly gluten sensitive tend to tolerate it in moderation. At restaurants, look for sandwiches made with whole rye.

BARLEY is one of the most ancient cultivated grains. Although it's supposed to be soothing to the intestines, it is also very acid-forming in the body.

OATS stabilize blood sugar, reduce cholesterol, and soothe the intestines and nervous system. Not usually encountered at dinner, they're most commonly served for breakfast as oatmeal or **as a** major component of granola and muesli. Oats also appear in some baked goods.

NON-GLUTEN GRAINS

RICE is the richest in B vitamins of all the grains and is served at all types of restaurants. It comes in numerous varieties: Short-grain brown rice, which is central to the macrobiotic diet, is perhaps the most nutritious form, whereas white rice (especially the aromatic basmati) is more common than brown in Indian and Asian cuisine. Nowadays, though, most establishments offer a choice of brown or white. Brown is best; 70 percent of the nutrients and all of the fiber in white rice are lost in refining. In addition, steamed or boiled rice is preferable to fried; the latter contains damaged cooking oil.

CORN often comes from genetically modified crops, so always ask if it is organic. It turns up in restaurants as corn on the cob, as a side vegetable and in corn bread. Italian or upscale restaurants sometimes serve polenta, a mush of cornmeal usually offered as a side dish or appetizer.

BUCKWHEAT—usually in the form of the Russian staple kasha or in Japanese soba noodles—is one of a few commercial crops not routinely sprayed because it has its own natural resistance. With the longest transit time in the gut of all the grains, it is the most filling and stabilizing for blood sugar. And pre-roasting transforms buckwheat into one of the few alkalizing grains; kasha is essentially pre-roasted buckwheat.

QUINOA was a major grain for the Incas of South America. A relative newcomer to the restaurant scene, its mild taste and fluffy texture has made it enormously popular. And it's rich in high-quality protein, making it a favorite with vegetarians. If you're not familiar with quinoa, try it as an alternative to rice or oatmeal.

AMARANTH is currently not widely available in restaurants, but it is becoming increasingly popular. I recommend it to clients because it's very nutritious and contains many good amino acids such as lysine, which is low in several other grains.

MILLET, a cereal grass sometimes used in the U.S. as birdseed, but in all kinds of dishes in Asia and Africa, is another excellent option. It is alkaline, easily digested and very nutritious with a high silica content for healthy skin and bones.

Legumes

They're the punch line of bad jokes, true, but beans—as well as peas and lentils—confer many health benefits. Known as legumes, or pulses, they lower cholesterol, control blood-sugar imbalances and regulate bowel function. Low in fat (with the exception of soy beans), they're a good source of protein (especially for vegetarians and vegans), fiber and B vitamins. From a culinary perspective, herbs and spices marry well with the mild taste of legumes, which absorb the flavor of sauces and have a pleasant texture that adds bulk to any meal.

For a few susceptible individuals, abdominal gas and bloating result from eating beans, no matter how carefully they are prepared. But most of us need not avoid beans for fear of their antisocial effects. A good chef knows that most varieties of beans should be presoaked, rinsed and thoroughly cooked to break down their indigestible sugars and destroy their enzyme inhibitors (if they haven't come from a can). Here's the dish on beans:

Chickpeas, black beans, kidney beans, adzuki beans and lentils are among the legumes that crop up in numerous cultures where they have nourished humankind for millennia. For instance, chickpeas, also called garbanzo beans, are used to make the hummus and falafels of Mediterranean cuisine, as well as being popular in Indian curries; black beans are used in Mexican burritos; kidney beans are the legume of choice for chili; the adzuki bean is popular in macrobiotic restaurants; and red lentils often form the basis of dhal (dal, daal, dahl), an easily digested Indian puree.

SOY BEANS merit a lengthier discussion because they're eaten so frequently and used in so many ways—and, in particular, associated with numerous health claims and controversies.

Asians have been including soy foods in their diets for thousands of years, a fact that's often touted as the main reason for Asians' longevity and low rates of certain cancers and other Western diseases. However, this may have more to do with the paucity of dairy and meat in the Asian diet, as well as the emphasis on vegetables and various lifestyle factors. The truth is that soy has never been eaten in large quantities in Asia. Note the miso soup in Japanese restaurants, in which only a few cubes of tofu float around. And next time you order Chinese vegetables with soy-bean curd, observe how the vegetables and rice predominate. This marginal role for soy stands in stark contrast to the modern soy burger at the center of the vegetarian entrée.

Over the past few decades, vegetarians and vegans in particular have become overreliant on soy because it is a balanced protein and can be formed into mock meat. Restaurants dutifully offer soy, often in the form of tofu, as the vegetarian option for protein.

However, studies detailing soy's high nutrient content and positive effects have recently been contested by additional research. Worse, soy is known to block the absorption of some nutrients and is thought to increase the likelihood of ovarian and breast cancer. For more information, check out *The Whole Soy Story: The Dark Side of America's Favorite Health Food* by Dr. Kaayla Daniel; the book investigates the health problems linked to the overconsumption of soy.

One solution is simply to cut back. Another is to be mindful of the kinds of soy products you consume. Organic, non-GMO soy is your best bet, as are soy products like miso, soy yogurt, natto and tempeh, all of which undergo a fermentation process in which otherwise non-viable nutrients are partly predigested—and phytates and enzyme inhibitors that cause gastric distress are neutralized. In addition, those forms of soy are endowed with probiotics. With the possible exception of soy yogurt, these healthy forms of soy are usually available in Chinese, Japanese and macrobiotic restaurants.

Tofu, perhaps the most ubiquitous form of soy in restaurants, provides some nutrition but should be eaten in moderation since it hasn't undergone the all-important fermentation process. As for edamame, it's a whole food but not easy to digest—good for you, but not in excess, that is.

Soy milk, soy ice cream and soy cheese, however, are highly processed and not fermented—best consumed only on occasion. They usually come with additives of one kind or another, in an attempt to mimic the flavor and texture of the real thing.

Desserts made from hemp, almonds or rice are better choices. There's even an amazing raw, vegan ice cream made from cashews and sweetened with agave in New York State, available at organicnectars.com; persuade your neighborhood chef to place an order. Raw-food restaurants are likely to place this ice cream—or perhaps the chef's own creation—on the dessert menu.

A soy product that should be completely avoided whenever possible is textured vegetable (or soy) protein, also known as TVP, which in similar forms goes by the names protein soy isolate or hydrolyzed plant (or soy) protein. Made from soybean meal after the oil has been processed out with chemicals and intense pressure, TVP is used in veggie burgers and fake meats. TVP, soy isolate and hydrolyzed soy bear a close chemical resemblance to plastic and may contain residues from processing, including petroleum solvents, sulphuric acids, hydrochloric acid and caustic soda. Those are just a few good reasons to bypass that fake turkey sandwich in favor of the Tempeh Reuben.

MEAT STILL ENJOYS A reputation as being as all-American as the Wild West and cowboy boots. But improving yourself is an all-American quality, too, and to do that it's best to cut down on your intake of animal products, including fish, meat, poultry, dairy and eggs. I'm not saying that you have to become vegetarian or vegan, though; each individual should do what's best for his or her body.

THE FOURTH PRECEPT:

If you choose to eat animal products, consume only (a) high-quality and sustainably raised animals (ideally pasture-raised and grass-fed, but at least hormone and antibiotic-free); and do so (b) in moderation—meaning smaller portions with less frequency.

Remember how proponents of The China Study argue that meat-eating is a leading cause of human disease, but followers of the nutritionist Weston A. Price say that it can be beneficial? That's not the only area of contention regarding animal products. Another is over whether animal fats cause heart disease. An increasingly vocal minority of researchers claim that the cholesterol myth is just that—a myth. They believe that highly processed vegetable oils and hydrogenated fats are more artery-clogging and lead to more heart trouble than lard. Of course, adherents of veganism and vegetarianism eschew animal products for a variety of reasons, while others believe that those diets are lacking in some essential nutrients such as vitamins B12 and D.

Different people will side with different research; your genetic makeup or lifestyle may mean that eating meat is necessary for your body to function smoothly. To figure it out, I advocate experimenting and also thinking about how certain foods and dietary principles make you feel.

If you consume animal products, I hope that you do so in moderation. Why? Well, for one thing, animal products are higher in protein than necessary for human health, creating more acidity than the body can process and leading to problems like fatigue and osteoporosis. In addition, there's substantial evidence that the practice of raising animals for human consumption—especially in conventional corporate feedlots—is unsustainable and environmentally problematic. Easy ways to lower the percentage of animal products in your diet include thinking of meat as a side dish rather than a main course, as well as eating smaller portions less frequently.

In addition, make sure that all of the animal products you consume— beef, dairy, eggs, chicken and so on—come from high-quality, organic and pasture-fed animals. As well as having no fiber, animal products are a concentrated source of the medications, stress, hormones and environmental toxins that the animal has been exposed to. That's a powerful argument for choosing an organic, pasture-fed animal, which won't have been subjected to stressful conditions or injected with toxins like hormones and antibiotics. Instead, it will have been raised similarly to the way it would have been in the wild: A pasture-raised cow, for instance, grazes on grass, gets exercise and is exposed to the sun, all of which results in a healthy cow—and extra benefits for us.

> **REMINDER: DON'T NECESSARILY WORRY ABOUT ORGANIC CERTIFICATION**
>
> Small farmers who raise animals sustainably and hormone and antibiotic-free often can't afford to obtain the accreditation "certified organic."

To summarize: Make sure that the animal products you eat are high quality and organic (that is, hormone- and antibiotic-free) and preferably grass-fed. In addition, consume them less often and in small portions—and eat them with vegetables (especially leafy greens) to counteract some of the potential negative effects. By making those tweaks, you ensure that high-quality meat, fish, poultry, dairy and eggs can become a healthy part of a balanced diet rather than a risk factor. In the following two sections, I round up the different kinds of animal foods appearing on restaurant menus.

Meat and Fish

Not all meats are created equal. Some are organic, some not; some grilled, others fried. Part of the purpose of this section is to further clarify and help you choose the healthiest options.

For instance, grilled or roasted meats are better for you than deep-fried dishes. (Be aware, though, that meats smoked or barbecued on charcoal grills can develop a carcinogen called polycyclic aromatic hydrocarbons.) Like most other foods, meat is best for your body when it has been cooked briefly and gently. Prolonged, high heat reduces the amount of vitamins and minerals in meat and denatures its protein. Worse, it increases the toxicity of contaminants already there, such as nitrates and pesticides. Of course, with the disease-causing pathogens showing up in animal products, it may not be such a bad idea to avoid rare or raw meat (which otherwise would be the healthiest way to consume high-quality, properly raised animal products). However, when possible, ask that your meat not be overcooked. Medium-rare is a good option and usually what chefs prefer anyway.

TIP: FOOD-COMBINING

Some foods digest well when eaten with specific kinds of dishes, while other foods are the opposite—concentrated starches and concentrated proteins, for instance, should be eaten separately. The idea behind food-combining is to eat the former category of foods together, and to separate the latter. Protein causes the body to produce specific enzymes and hydrochloric acid, which increases the stomach's acidity; starches need an alkaline environment for digestion. Translation: Eating a lot of meat with starches like bread or potatoes can cause gas and indigestion. A food-combining solution: Pair heavy proteins like meat with vegetables, such as leafy greens, instead of with starches like breads, grains and potatoes.

Here are details about the different types of meats you're likely to encounter on menus:

BEEF is a source of iron and vitamin B12, as well as essential fats. Cows raised in pastures—where they're exposed to the sun and eat grass—provide the healthiest meat; in fact, an essential fat and anti-cancer nutrient called conjugated linoleic acid (CLA) occurs only in grass-fed animals.

One rung down from grass-fed cows is organic beef, which means that the animal has been raised without hormones and antibiotics, but has been fed grains, corn or organic vegetarian feed. Often this is for taste reasons but sometimes even these animals are overfed in an attempt to fatten them up, a practice that makes them more prone to disease. Since grass is the natural diet for cows, animals that eat grains or corn—even if it's high-quality organic—are not as healthy as their grass-fed counterparts and therefore not as healthy for humans.

And as far as factory-farmed beef goes, I advise avoiding it altogether because of the health, environmental and moral issues involved. Jammed together in pens where they never see sunlight and are injected with hormones and who knows what else, the cows raised in such farms are usually very sick—part of the reason they're injected with excess antibiotics. That's an excellent reason to opt for grass-fed, sustainably raised beef; or, at the very least, a hormone and antibiotic-free animal.

And think of the fact that it may be a tad pricey as a motivator for you to eat less meat overall—as you may recall, I'm a big proponent of eating meat in moderation.

CHICKEN, LAMB and **PORK**, all sources of protein, can be good for you, like beef, if you choose an organic, naturally raised animal and eat it in moderation.

When it comes to pork, though, don't be fooled by the advertising ("The New White Meat"). It's actually probably less healthy for you than chicken or lamb. And it makes such a difference to your health that I'll say it again: Order free-range, naturally fed chicken, lamb or pork—and consume small portions.

GAME ANIMALS like boar and venison are among the healthiest kinds of meats because they come from freshly killed animals that lived in the wild. These animals are leaner than beef or chicken and boast a higher proportion of omega-3 fatty acids. In addition, they're less likely to be contaminated or diseased. It is becoming easier to find boar and venison in trendy restaurants, as well as establishments emphasizing organic dishes, although, for some, venison's gamey flavor is an acquired taste.

CURED MEATS like sausages, luncheon meats and bacon can be okay to eat in moderation; it all comes down to how they are raised and made. I recommend cutting out luncheon meats altogether—nearly all of them contain carcinogenic preservatives such as nitrates. If you can't stay away from, say, bologna, at least get a package labeled "nitrate-free." Two requirements should be met before you purchase bacon or sausage: (1) The meat should have come from a good-quality animal, one that was naturally raised and fed (hormone- and antibiotic-free). (2) The way the meat was made should be as natural as possible. Sausage without casings or fillers, produced on the premises at an organic restaurant, for instance, gets my thumbs-up—as long as you eat it in moderation.

FOIE GRAS and **VEAL** tend to be served only in upscale restaurants; the former is the liver of a fattened-up goose or duck, and the latter is the meat of a milk-fed (or sometimes formula-fed) baby calf.

A lot of people avoid veal and foie gras (French for "fat liver") for moral reasons. Since I don't see any particular health benefits from eating either of these foods, I recommend avoiding them altogether.

COLD-WATER FISH like salmon, mackerel, cod and sardines, are chock-full of heart-healthy omega 3 fatty acids as well as fat-soluble vitamins and minerals, including iodine. Unfortunately, these goodies are meaningless if the fish is conventionally farm-raised, a technique that results in more PCBs, mercury and disease—and fewer omega 3's. Plus, the feed for farmed salmon usually contains dye to give the flesh a pink color.

If you want the benefits of organically farm-raised or wild fish, salmon—a potent source of omega 3—is probably the easiest fish to find at restaurants. Most nutritious in its raw form (for instance, as sushi), it's also healthy when steamed or baked. Skip tempura, though; it involves dipping fish in batter before deep-frying it in hot oil.

SCAVENGER FISH include tuna, swordfish, carp and catfish. They eat almost anything they find in the sea, including already-dead fish (yum!). That's why their tissues are likely to contain the toxins of other fish, like PCBs and mercury; it's also why scavenger fish are considered no-no's for women who are pregnant or breastfeeding. If you like fish, I suggest sticking mostly to the cold-water kind.

SHELLFISH is a category that includes scallops, clams, mussels, oysters, shrimp, crabs and lobsters. They should be eaten in moderation and always while very fresh and in season. For a number of reasons, I am not a huge fan. Shellfish spoil easily and are a common cause of food poisoning, as well as being prone to contamination. Be sure yours are sourced from clean waters.

To help you make quality seafood choices when you're shopping or out to eat, download the *Seafood Pocket Guide* at (http://edf.org/documents/1980_pocket_seafood_selector.pdf). It lists fish both high in omega-3 fats and low in environmental contaminants.

Dairy and Eggs

Cheese conjures up sophisticated images like wine-and-cheese parties, while milk perhaps sounds quaint (think milkmen in the 1950s). Like those varying images, dairy and eggs have varying effects on your health, depending on who you are, how much you eat and the quality of what you consume. Frankly, I'm not the biggest advocate of consuming a lot of dairy, but I try to stay open-minded.

Dairy's big selling point is that it's a source of calcium. Yet milk's acidity means that it actually leaches calcium from the bones. In addition, its low magnesium content in relation to its calcium (they are required in balance for proper utilization) means that the calcium may not get completely used by the body. It's better obtained from vegetables, seeds and nuts.

Another reason I'm not a big fan of dairy products is their tendency to create mucus in the body, resulting in anything from a runny nose to a clogged-up digestive system.

In addition, many people are lactose intolerant; only around a third of the world's population possesses the genetic mutation required for the proper digestion of dairy. Asian and African-American populations include an especially high percentage of milk-intolerant individuals, which is why you're not likely to find many dairy products on the menu at an Asian restaurant.

That doesn't mean dairy is the devil, at least not for people who digest it well—as long as you get it from grass-fed cows, or at minimum, opt for an organic version. I recommend avoiding products containing Recombinant Bovine Growth Hormone, aka RBGH, a genetically engineered drug associated with growth abnormalities and malignant tumors. Another reason to go organic: Dairy cows fed unnatural diets, forced to produce excessive quantities of milk, confined to small stalls or kept in unhygienic conditions often suffer from infected udders. This infection, called mastitis, causes the sick cows to release pus into their milk.

A roundup of dairy products commonly found in restaurants follows.

MILK itself doesn't feature prominently on most menus, but it crops up in sauces, smoothies and as a side dish for tea and coffee. Even so, cow's milk contains more protein than we need and can cause weight gain. Some organic-focused restaurants offer preferable alternatives like rice, almond or hemp milk (note that I didn't include soy, which I'll address in an upcoming section); ask the staff if you don't see any of those options on the menu.

CHEESE is often a concentrated form of milk, best eaten in moderation. Some of my clients who want to reduce their cheese consumption find it extremely hard to do so; cheese is considered one of the most difficult foods to stop eating (in addition to sugar) because of its casein, a protein with addictive qualities.

One partial solution is to eat better types of cheese, like raw (unpasteurized) versions, which retain more enzymes and nutrients, and boast an arguably better taste than their pasteurized counterparts. Although they're not yet common in the United States, with demand, their availability is increasing, particularly in restaurants that stress organic or specialty foods.

Sheep and goat cheeses are another smart alternative. Easier to digest than cheese made from cow's milk, these cheeses are increasingly popular in restaurants, where you might find them atop salads and as sandwich fillings

And no surprise here: I recommend avoiding processed cheese, a staple in some sandwiches and fast-food entrées; they usually contain additives such as emulsifiers, extenders, phosphates and hydrogenated oils. You'll likely find them easy to give up, considering their bland taste and plastic texture.

CULTURED DAIRY PRODUCTS—kefir, yogurt and sour cream—are easier to digest than other dairy items because their lactose and casein are already partially broken down. Kefir is a liquid yogurt traditionally created from camel's milk, although many versions use cow's milk. Most Greek and Indian restaurants serve yogurt; the latter may also use ghee in food preparation. Well tolerated by most people, ghee is butter with the milk solids removed.

BUTTER most often appears at your table accompanying a complimentary basket of bread. Unless you have a dairy allergy, a moderate amount of butter—especially organic—offers some benefits, including easily digested fats and the fat-soluble vitamins A and D.

ICE CREAM and **CREAM** populate the dessert section of many menus. Practice moderation, or try some of the naturally sweetened nut-based ice creams popping up at raw-food restaurants.

EGGS are often classified with dairy products (especially by vegetarians) because, like milk and cheese, they come from animals but the animals don't have to be killed to obtain the food. Rich in vitamins, minerals and protein, eggs can be quite nourishing.

> **TIP:**
> **EAT THE WHOLE EGG**
>
> Egg whites contain an enzyme inhibitor that's neutralized by the yolk. So don't eat only the whites—eat the whole shebang, yolk and whites. Your digestion will thank you.

Their cholesterol content causes debate, however; overcooked, it becomes oxidized, meaning it transforms from a useful nutrient into a potentially harmful chemical. For that reason (i.e., they contain oxidized cholesterol), avoid powdered eggs, which have been through a heating and drying process. To avoid oxidation in your egg order, ask for lightly poached or sunny-side-up eggs rather than scrambled or fried; similarly, soft-boiled trumps hard-boiled. Raw eggs are even more beneficial than the lightly cooked kind. However, people susceptible to salmonella, such as the elderly, the infirm or pregnant women, should avoid raw eggs.

As with dairy and meat, a chef's choice of egg supplier has implications for both nutritional quality and taste. Battery-caged hens tend to turn out eggs with salmonella, few nutrients and a bland or fishy taste—and the cruelty of crowding hens together is another reason to skip ordering such eggs. Free-range, pasture-raised hens, on the other hand, produce unpredictable eggs; as with heirloom vegetables, the result is a richer flavor and increased nutrient content. At the very least, stick with hormone and antibiotic-free eggs taken from cage-free hens.

IN THE NEXT SECTION, I discuss the kinds of things that make your mouth water—sweeteners, seasonings, fats and oils, and beverages. These more subtle foods may be potentially harmful, but they don't have to be, as long as you approach these full-of-flavor foods the right way. Which brings me to my final premise, one that by now you know, but which I'd like to highlight once more.

THE FIFTH PRECEPT: To feel better immediately, simply reduce your intake of artificial, chemical-laden processed foods as well as sugar, caffeine and alcohol.

As you read through the next few categories, keep this precept in mind. It's actually less difficult to follow than you might think; stick to the natural flavorings, not the substances created in a test tube. Do those long, chemical, hard-to-pronounce names even sound that tasty? Not really, right? Educating yourself about all of the tasty *and* natural substances out there (honey, anyone?) is the perfect insurance against being lured away by processed foods.

Fats and Oils

They've got a less-than-savory rep, but don't be afraid of fats and oils. They play an important role in the human diet.

It's fats and oils that slow the release of sugar from other foods, create a feeling of satisfaction, give us a source of energy and allow us to absorb fat-soluble vitamins, including A, D, E and K by carrying them across the gut wall. In addition, our bodies use fats as building materials, incorporating them into the cell membranes to create the right balance between firmness and flexibility.

We like to preach about its evils—weight gain, heart disease—while still associating fatty food with comfort and fun. Truth is, it can get kind of complicated, so let's simplify. The list of different fats and oils is a long one, so here's what you need to know about the ones you are most likely to encounter at a restaurant.

Trans fats or hydrogenated oils, made by injecting hydrogen into liquid vegetable oils to make them more solid, should be completely avoided as they are probably the most harmful ingredient in our food supply. In fact, New York City has ensured you'll avoid these oils because in 2008, the city banned the use of trans fats in restaurants. So it is far less likely than before that dining out will mean consuming damaged vegetable oils in the form of vegetable shortening and hydrogenated margarine.

Avocados, raw nuts and seeds, coconuts and olives should form the bulk of your fat intake and are excellent sources of essential fatty acids, fiber and other co-factors (when these foods are turned into oils, some of these goodies are eliminated). These plant fats should not cause weight gain as part of a balanced diet, nor should they contribute to heart disease.

Whole coconut meat is preferable to coconut oil or coconut butter, although those latter two don't deserve the artery-blocking image painted by some, even though they are a saturated fat. Want to learn more? Take a look at *The Healing Properties of Coconut Oil* by nutritionist Bruce Fife.

HEMP SEEDS and FLAXSEEDS are valued for their essential fatty acids, but they are best used whole and raw since processing, storage and heating can turn these delicate oils rancid. Flax contains more omega 3 than fish (minus contaminants such as mercury and PCBs), but you can't cook with flax oil—it's best to eat the seeds. Hemp and flax oils are healthy only when cold-pressed; in that form, they make an excellent salad dressing.

OLIVE OIL is a monounsaturated fat. Even though it has negligible amounts of essential fatty acids, it's better than many other oils and doesn't contain a high amount of harmful omega 6. And the form in which it's served at most quality restaurants—as salad dressing—is good, since it has more benefits when raw, especially if it's extra virgin, organic and cold-pressed. It crops up in that form at Italian and Mediterranean establishments. Like most oils, though, olive oil is damaged by high heat.

BUTTER has become cool again after the downfall of margarine because of its dangerous levels of trans fat (hydrogenated oils). I believe butter—especially organic butter from a grass-fed cow—has some health benefits when consumed in moderation. Margarine, on the other hand, can damage your arteries more than any amount of butterfat because of its aforementioned trans fats. Its overuse in recent years—along with oils like soy, sunflower and corn—has contributed to a national over-consumption of omega 6 fats versus omega 3, a situation that has been linked to numerous health problems.

Salt and Seasonings

My friends like to tease that I have a "salt tooth" in contrast to most people's "sweet tooth," but I've learned to treat salt as I would sugar—with fondness but also caution.

Salt provides sodium, an important mineral involved in many bodily processes. However, it's unhealthy when you're getting a lot of sodium but hardly any potassium, a mineral found mainly in fresh fruits and vegetables. That's because sodium and potassium work together as intimate partners. It is essential that they remain in proper balance for the smooth functioning of our muscles, lungs, heart and nervous system, as well as for the water balance within our bodies. In particular, many people suffer from raised blood pressure, muscle cramps and water retention when they consume too much salt.

Most people get *way* more than enough salt whether they try to or not, just because salt, and therefore sodium, is overabundant in our modern, processed meals. Potassium, however, is lacking, because we don't eat enough vegetables. We need less than half a teaspoon of sodium per day, but many of us are consuming *seven* times that amount.

At a restaurant, you can request that your meal be prepared with less salt. You'll be amazed at how quickly you lose the desire for excess salt and start to find too much unappealing—I certainly have, despite my "salt tooth."

TIP: GOOD SALT SUBSTITUTES

One clever and healthful way to reduce your sodium intake at a restaurant is to ask for extra garlic, ginger, herbs or spices to be substituted instead, a move that will increase the flavor of your meal while adding some health benefits. Some of the best additions are garlic, a natural antibiotic; ginger, an anti-inflammatory and digestive aid; cayenne, a circulation enhancer; turmeric, an antioxidant and anti-inflammatory; and green herbs such as parsley or cilantro, a good source of vitamins and chlorophyll.

REFINED TABLE SALT tends to be processed and altered with chemicals—it's sodium chloride with no nutritional benefits. I recommend deleting it from your diet, since it contributes to the sodium-potassium imbalance described above, and usually contains aluminum to boot.

KOSHER SALT is a coarse salt with no additives; its thick crystal grains help to cure meat, thus its name (since it's used by some Jews to make meat kosher). Foodies like this salt for its texture and taste; perhaps because it appears in gourmet foods, it's sometimes thought to be healthier than table salt. That's not the case, however; there's no nutritional difference between table and kosher salt (the latter may be marginally more healthful because it doesn't have additives, but don't be fooled into thinking it's good for you).

SEA SALT or **HIMALAYAN CRYSTAL SALT** both appear at some restaurants and are fine to eat in moderation. Natural and unprocessed, they contain minerals from the ocean, have a better flavor than table salt and tend to be prized by good chefs. Although sea and crystal salt are gaining in popularity, they're still currently most likely to crop up in the kitchens of health-food or gourmet restaurants. At raw-food restaurants, they're usually the only kind of salt offered.

BRAGG'S LIQUID AMINOS is a low-sodium alternative to soy sauce (although it's made from soy beans) that appears on the tables of many health-food restaurants. Although it's better than table salt, I tend not to think of it as a health food. Despite its name, the amount of amino acids (i.e., protein) that it provides is negligible. And like soy sauce, it has been found to contain some naturally occurring monosodium glutamate (MSG), a flavor-enhancer that has been associated with various health problems. Nevertheless, it does add a strong, savory flavor to meals.

SHOYU and **TAMARI**, both commonly referred to as soy sauce, are more or less interchangeable; both are fermented soy condiments, except that tamari is wheat-free. Asian and health-food restaurants serve shoyu and tamari, where they're sometimes also used for stir-frying. Health conscious diners prefer naturally brewed versions over highly processed and additive-laden cheaper imitations. However, I find soy sauce a questionable substitute for table salt because of the soy, wheat and the inevitable processing. Unless stated on the label, soy sauce is not a low-sodium alternative and is best used sparingly.

Sweeteners

"You're sweet." "How sweet it is." "That's *sweet*." The English language is peppered with instances of how, well, *sweet* sweetness is. So it's understandable that sugary foods are where I get the most resistance and guilt from my clients.

It's not exactly a news flash that refined white sugar and the more insidious high fructose corn syrup is bad for us. It's difficult to get away from, though, because sugar is in all kinds of foods—not just bottled drinks and desserts, but also savory sauces.

Even if we're aware of which foods contain refined white sugar, it's hard not to order them anyway. That's because sugar is addictive. Stop eating it and you'll experience withdrawal symptoms. Eat some and you will crave more. Sounds like an addiction to me. (Then there's the emotional aspect of sugar cravings. Consider how children are offered sweets if they're "good" or "behave.") To make matters worse, it seems that we have been biologically programmed to seek out sweetness as a way to avoid poison, which tends to be bitter. But I bet evolution intended for us to eat fruits and not, say, doughnuts.

Even though you know that sweets are bad for you, it's worth pointing out the many ways they're bad. Sugar is an anti-nutrient, not only giving the body zero nutrition, but actually robbing us of goodies. Plus, it's probably the major contributor to weight gain; at a certain point of saturation, the body converts it to fat, putting excess sugar into storage in order to quickly remove it from the blood where it would otherwise create havoc. After all, there is only so much sugar that we can use as energy. Sugar has been linked to a variety of other ailments, from lowered immunity and poor gut flora to cancer and diabetes.

Yet, according to the USDA, we are eating increasingly more sugar. The average American consumes over a cup a day of the stuff—an increase of 23 percent between 1985 and 1999.

So what should we do? Well, we have to be really smart about our approach. Something I have noticed with my clients is that once they begin to take better care of themselves in other areas of their lives and eat better-quality foods, their cravings tend to lessen. Sometimes exercise helps, as does eating a little more protein and drinking more water. I always suggest a switch to more natural, gentler forms of sweeteners. Take these steps and over time you will gradually experience refined sugar as being too sweet and tasting fake. True, it may take a while, but I've found that this approach has worked, not only for me but for many former sugar addicts with whom I've worked.

Let's take a look at some of the common sweeteners you will encounter at restaurants.

WHITE TABLE SUGAR, HIGH FRUCTOSE CORN SYRUP and even **BROWN SUGAR** should be avoided as much as possible.

ORGANIC RAW CANE SUGAR, FLORIDA CRYSTALS and **TURBINADO SUGAR** have gained in popularity and are commonly found on the tables and in desserts at health-food restaurants. Although I am not a big fan and don't use them myself, I believe they are a slightly better option than the completely refined stuff, since these kinds of sugars do retain some nutrients and are better for the environment. But they're not healthy.

MAPLE SYRUP and **BROWN RICE SYRUP** are preferable to all of the above. They are the most commonly consumed natural sweeteners. While not ideal because they can negatively impact existing digestive issues and have a fairly high glycemic index, they are okay in moderation if they are pure and of a high quality.

HONEY is a far better choice than many of the other sweeteners, especially the raw, unheated varieties, which are rich in antioxidants, enzymes and various healing co-factors.

RAW AGAVE NECTAR is fast becoming the sweetener of choice among those in the know. It boasts a delicious sugarlike flavor, as well as having negligible effects on blood sugar (it's deemed safe for diabetics) and being rich in vitamins and minerals.

STEVIA (technically a supplement), extracted from the sweet leaves of the stevia plant, is also becoming increasingly popular for its highly sugary taste and safeness for diabetics, although some people are not crazy about its aftertaste. In addition, although it has been used safely by humans for a long time, there is conflicting research in regard to its safety.

More and more restaurants are providing agave and stevia for tea or coffee, as well as using them in place of sugar in desserts and baked goods

ARTIFICIAL SWEETENERS like Splenda, Equal or NutraSweet (aspartame) should be avoided. There are more adverse reactions to NutraSweet reported to the FDA than to all other foods and additives combined. Plus, there is even convincing evidence that these artificial sweeteners lead to weight gain.

Beverages

A sparkling stream of water runs through a picturesque valley. This could be an ad for anything from beer to an energy drink. The point? Advertisers know that we know that water is good for us. So they use it to sell beverages that aren't so good. Read on for details about the drinks you'll find at restaurants.

WATER should be your beverage of choice, in my opinion; usually it's the most natural and purest liquid you can get. Bottled water in restaurants tends to be overpriced, but it may be worth it if the only other option is unfiltered tap water, which will be polluted by chlorine and fluoride, among other contaminants. Filtered tap water is the best option: It's free, safe and better for the environment than bottled water (plus, you avoid ingesting chemicals that may leach into the water from the plastic bottle). If the restaurant's water is filtered, the food that's cooked in it will be safer for you as well.

> **TIP: WATER TEMPERATURE**
>
> Room-temperature water is the healthiest kind. That's because ice-cold water is difficult to digest, so ask for yours with no ice—but with a slice of lemon, which makes the water more alkalizing and cleansing.

FRUIT JUICES are okay to drink but quite sugary, which is why I recommend diluting them with water. **VEGETABLE JUICES**: much better. They count toward your nutrient intake, especially with dark greens thrown in.

SODAS and **SOFT DRINKS** are composed of unfiltered, artificially carbonated water with added sugar (or, worse, corn syrup or artificial sweeteners), flavorings, colorings, preservatives and sometimes caffeine. In addition, their high phosphoric-acid content is associated with osteoporosis. Not a recipe for health. I recommend avoiding them altogether, especially the diet ones, which are loaded with artificial sweeteners that, research has suggested, actually may cause weight gain.

As long as they're sweetened with fruit juice instead of cane sugar, natural sodas are fine to drink in moderation, since they're made from cleaner water and are caffeine-free.

> **TIP: ELECTROLYTES FOR ATHLETES**
>
> Looking to replenish those electrolytes after a tough workout? Replace your Gatorade with coconut water. It's loaded with electrolytes and a naturally sweet taste to boot.

COFFEE, provided by most restaurants, can provide a much-needed lift. Still, my recommendation is to reduce caffeine consumption with the goal of eventually giving it up altogether. Sure, coffee beans may contain antioxidants; plus, some people metabolize caffeine better than others. However, caffeine in general, and coffee in particular, is linked to raised blood pressure, insomnia, nervous conditions, osteoporosis and certain cancers. At the very least, imbibing caffeine with your meal reduces the availability of minerals in the food—it leaches them out.

If you can't resist ordering a cup, check whether the restaurant offers an organic, fair-trade or shade-grown version.

GREEN TEA may be the most healthful, or at least the most benign, of all caffeinated beverages. That's because it contains polyphenols, a type of antioxidant that can reduce blood pressure (note coffee's opposite effect), lower blood fats and combat those free radicals we encounter in a city environment. It contains much less caffeine than coffee. In addition, it has theanine, which mitigates some of caffeine's effects to produce a calmer type of energy and prevents a caffeine "hangover."

BLACK TEA has fewer antioxidants and more caffeine than green. But it doesn't contain as much caffeine as coffee, unless it is steeped for an especially long time.

Both green and black tea come from the same plant, often one that's been heavily sprayed, so seek out an organic version.

DECAFFEINATED TEA or **COFFEE** is fine to drink if the caffeine has been removed using the Swiss-water process. Otherwise, residue from chemicals used to remove the caffeine might remain—a non-issue if the product is certified organic. And note that all decaffeinated beverages still contain some traces of caffeine.

HERBAL TEAS may be the best hot drink overall, since they are naturally caffeine-free and boast mild therapeutic benefits. For instance, peppermint and ginger tea both are helpful to drink after a heavy meal, since they aid digestion; chamomile, as you probably know, has calming properties.

FERMENTED DRINKS are digestive aids, rich in enzymes and probiotics. They tend to be offered by establishments that focus on traditional health foods. Kombucha tea is not technically a tea, but rather a fermented cold drink made by steeping a mushroomlike growth in water. Rich in enzymes, probiotics and B vitamins, kombucha is a wonderful aid to digestion and general well-being. A "live" product, this tea is popular in raw- and health-food restaurants. Other common kinds of fermented drinks include amazake, made from rice; kefir, which is lacto-fermented milk; and ginger ale and apple cider, both healthy when made using old-fashioned methods.

WINE is fermented, true, but I believe that its alcohol content tends to neutralize the much-touted health benefits. Although wine has been in the news as being good for you in various small ways, my experience is that people use that as an excuse to drink too much. Even in relatively small amounts, wine is an anti-nutrient, particularly good at robbing the body of B vitamins. All alcohol can make you accident prone, dehydrated, unable to concentrate and even aggressive. It should be avoided if you are susceptible to candida overgrowth. And it's worth repeating: Long-term drinking to excess, whether labeled alcoholism or not, can result in liver damage and stomach ulcers, not to mention a host of social and emotional problems.

Still, like coffee, alcohol can be useful in moderation. After a stressful day at work, a relaxing glass of wine can make all the difference to your enjoyment of a meal and your ability to converse with fellow diners. Plus, it can stimulate the digestive process. Red wine in particular provides some antioxidant benefits and is said to be good for the heart in moderate amounts. As with coffee, though, there is no need to rely on wine for your antioxidants; think vegetables and fruits instead.

If you do choose to consume alcohol, organic beer or red wine is the best choice; like other organic goods, these drinks should be free of pesticides. And biodynamic wine is arguably better than regular organic, since biodynamic producers go to extraordinary lengths to create special, pure growing conditions.

Restaurants with an extensive wine list may offer one labeled sulphite-free or NSA, meaning "no sulphites added." Sulphites occur naturally on grapes, but many vineyards add more to prevent bacterial growth, oxidation and a vinegary taste. Many people experience allergic side effects, including headaches, when they consume sulphites, and some connoisseurs prefer the taste of a low-sulphite wine. White wine generally has fewer sulphites than red.

BEER, **ALE** and **LAGER** are lower in alcohol than wine, but it's still important to watch the amount that you drink.

HARD LIQUOR or **SPIRITS** such as vodka, tequila, or rum are much higher in alcohol than both wine and beer, which is why they're often diluted with tonic water or fruit juice. Be especially careful of these because of the high alcohol content.

IN PRACTICE:
MAKING IT ALL WORK

I'M NOT THE KIND of guy to just hand you the facts and run. What do you do now that I've provided an education about different foods? Well, first let's remind ourselves what those *Five Precepts* are:

1. There's no one right way to eat for everyone.
2. The overwhelming majority of your diet should consist of natural, high-quality and whole foods.
3. Everyone would be better off if a larger proportion of their diet consisted of plants—mostly vegetables (in particular, leafy greens), and some nuts, seeds and fruits.
4. If you choose to eat animal products, consume only (a) high-quality and sustainably raised animals (ideally pasture-raised and grass-fed, but at least hormone and antibiotic-free); and do so (b) in moderation—meaning smaller portions with less frequency.
5. To feel better immediately, simply reduce your intake of artificial, chemical-laden processed foods as well as sugar, caffeine and alcohol.

I want to make it easy for you to transition—and stick—to healthier dining, so here are several psychological and social tips for following the precepts outlined above.

The Right Approach
MOTIVATION

This is the *why*: You've got to know why you're doing something to be able to really carry it out.

So, why are you changing your diet? Okay, I confess. We all, including me, want to be slimmer, trimmer, better looking. And those are okay reasons. But there are better reasons, like heightened energy, greater strength, fewer illnesses and clearer thinking. I find that it helps to get excited about getting the most out of life and bringing enjoyment not only to yourself, but also to other people—not to mention planet earth, since our food choices have a major impact on the environment.

So, right now, take out a sheet of paper and write down *why* you want to eat healthier. Once you've written down your motivations, commit to them—that is, setting a clear intention. It's a great launchingpad for getting—and staying —motivated.

The other part of intention and motivation? Believing that, yes, you can do this. Don't simply hope you can succeed; know that you will.

AWARENESS

Awareness means (a) remembering your motivation (your *why*) and intention (your commitment); and (b) being aware of the various forces that might act against you. Admitting that challenges exist is a necessary step to moving beyond them.

These challenges include: physical cravings and addictions, emotional attachments to food, cultural conditioning, advertising and a lack of education about healthy eating. Peer pressure is another biggie; you're going to need to keep your resolve if others try to coax you back to your old ways. Just be aware that change can make others uncomfortable.

Realize that these scenarios are not personal to you. They are issues for all of us, since we are all human and ever-evolving. Therefore, be aware that you are not a victim.

Awareness also means paying attention to how certain foods make us feel, physically and mentally. Keep a diet diary if that helps. Begin to eliminate any foods or drinks that drain your energy, give you indigestion, make you irritable or create so much guilt when you consume them that you simply don't enjoy or digest them properly.

> **YOUR CHOICES AS AN INDIVIDUAL**
>
> Part of being human is having the ability to make conscious choices based on our intentions and what is best for us.

PATIENCE

Do you wish I had a magic formula for positive change? Actually, I do. Think of it as the magical trio: patience, perseverance and resilience. Okay, I admit it: Those qualities aren't so simple.

In dietary terms, those words mean realizing that lasting improvements take time and application. At first you may need to be satisfied with eating healthier about half of the time, but once you do get to that 50/50 mark, you will have the momentum to go further, slowly, going from 60/40 to 70/30 and onward, until you may even hit 90/10. Don't be too extreme right away, though. Just start with the 50 percent rule and see what happens. En route, don't be discouraged by slip-ups. Just notice it and move on.

After a while, you'll notice that, bit by bit, you're starting to find excess sugar and salt unpalatable. In the meantime, instead of dwelling on what you need to eliminate, simply eat more of the good stuff so that it crowds out both the desire and the space for unhealthy foods.

Try not to be too rigid with yourself or others. People who are hard on themselves tend to be judgmental of others. That's counterproductive. If your mission to eat better becomes a strict chore and strains your relationships, it will make you miserable and longing for your old, comfortable ways. Remember what works for your body may not necessarily work for someone else's; that's bio-individuality.

How to Eat

Of course, I couldn't possibly lay down the rules of such a personal and elusive concept as "how to eat." Nevertheless, here are some helpful tips:

STAY NOURISHED: Stay on top of cravings by beginning the day with a sustaining breakfast and eating a nutritious lunch. Make lunch your largest meal of the day, and when possible eat dinner early and fairly light—a large salad or vegetarian option, for instance—so that you're not overeating close to bedtime. And keep hydrated all day by drinking water.

CHEW: Sounds obvious, but you'd be surprised how many people don't, at least not properly. Thorough mastication helps your body digest nutrients better. (To see just how little chewing we all do, try chewing 10 to 20 times per mouthful or until the food becomes liquid—not easy, right?)

EAT SLOWLY: Pause between bites to savor the flavors and check in with your stomach to ask it "are you full yet?" This will make your meal last longer, and help to prevent the discomfort and weight gain associated with overeating.

DON'T OVEREAT: Eating slowly and chewing properly helps to prevent this, but note how much you order in the first place. Practice portion control. And realize that it's unnecessary to order an appetizer and dessert as well as an entrée. If you're still hungry after eating slowly, you can always order more. Have a light fruit snack before going out to eat; if you arrive at a restaurant starving, you're likely to overeat. And skip the bread at the beginning of the meal.

AVOID DISTRACTIONS: If you're not good at blocking out extraneous noise and distractions, you might want to eat in silence or alone occasionally. But given that most meals—especially in restaurants— are a fun, shared experience, try to dine with people who don't give you indigestion. Keep heated debates to a minimum so that you can chew and assimilate the food properly. Reading and television are also distracting.

DON'T EAT UNDER STRESS: Anxiety and anger shut down the digestive function as part of the "fight or flight" response. Eating under such circumstances can cause indigestion. At such times you will be tempted to go for comfort foods or to overeat to numb your feelings. If you do arrive stressed at a restaurant, take a few deep breaths and remember your intention.

PRACTICE GRATITUDE: Be thankful for your food and for all the people and forces that brought it to your table: the sun that shone down on it, the farmer who grew it and the waiter who delivered it. Taking a moment to give thanks will calm you and remind you of your connection to the whole. It will also enable you to feel grateful for real, healthy food and simple pleasures.

ENJOY: Whatever you choose to eat — even if you know it is not perfectly healthy—allow yourself to enjoy it. Guilt is a stressor that makes you, and your digestive system, unhappy.

EXPERIMENT: It's that bio-individuality thing again. Experiment with different dietary theories and foods so that over time you can discover what works best for you and your body. At the very least, eat a few meals each week with no animal products by ordering proteins such as beans. Whatever you do, eat your veggies!

SOCIAL SITUATIONS

Even with the best intentions you will occasionally end up at a restaurant that does not serve healthy food and/or with a group of diners who do not share your dietary goals. What to do?

ORDER SIDES: Most restaurants have a selection of side dishes that you can create a meal out of, such as vegetables and a whole grain.

SPECIAL ORDER: An accommodating, creative chef will be happy to make something especially for you. Try requests like: "I know it's not on the menu, but could you put together a plate of vegetables and beans for me?" or "I'd like an extra-large version of your side salad as my entrée."

SKIP THE FREEBIES: Just because the bread is complimentary does not mean that you have to eat it. Likewise, try to ignore those fortune cookies or mints that arrive with the bill.

ASK FOR SAUCE ON THE SIDE: If the salad dressings and sauces are not up to par, ask for the waitstaff to bring them on the side so that you can monitor how much you use.

ASK FOR SUBSTITUTIONS: Some restaurants charge for doing this, and some don't. In any case, it is worth asking for things like green veggies or even boiled potatoes instead of french fries.

I hope to have left you with enough inspiration, motivation and education to put my five precepts into action. It's time to start enjoying your food more than ever while getting healthier at the same time. You *can* have your naturally sweetened dessert and eat it too. So let's get to the best part (I have a feeling you may have taken a peek already) and check out the restaurants.

Icon Key

Meals for 1 (including beverage, tax, and tip) under $10

$11–$30

$31–$60

above $60

Vegetarian menu

Flexatarian (good meat and vegetarian options)

Primarily meat-based menu

Vegan menu

Macrobiotic menu

Raw menu

Gluten-free options

Naturally sweetened desserts

Critics Pick

Nearby subways

THE RESTAURANTS

ANGELICA KITCHEN

Gourmet Vegan
300 E. 12th St. @ 2nd Ave.
L 6 R W
212 228-2909
angelicakitchen.com
11:30 am–10:30 pm daily
Cash only, BYOB

"Whole foods." "Slow foods." The words are thrown around with abandon these days. Happily enough, there's a little place in the East Village that gets both pretty much just right. Angelica Kitchen has been serving organic, vegan, Asian-inflected cuisine since 1976—long before it was trendy.

One caveat about the eatery: It gets packed, and it doesn't take reservations. Would-be diners must wait on a cushy seat in the foyer, eyeballing the rows of light wooden tables and hoping one becomes available. The fare is worth the wait, however. A fragrant bowl of "dashi and noodle" (a simple Japanese broth with soba noodles) swirls with seaweed, fresh ginger, soy sauce and silky shiitakes. Spoon up flavorful bites and savor the notion that everything is organic, most ingredients are fairly traded and sourced from small local farms, and extra food is donated to City Harvest. Take a sip of water—it's filtered here; in a pro-environment move, Angelica refuses to use bottles—and skip slightly bland vegetable sushi in favor of a simple "dragon bowl" of rice, beans, tofu, greens and a tangle of mineral-packed sea vegetables. The dish seems bland at first, but gains traction once various sauces are applied: "Gravy" based in a simple brown rice roux lends tofu a welcome spiciness, and brown rice becomes much more interesting under a drizzle of fresh carrot-ginger dressing. Angelica's broad menu features two gourmet vegan specials daily in addition to naturally sweetened, dairy-free desserts. Though fruit crumbles were nothing to write home about, we loved a delicate mint custard in a crunchy oat tart shell. A small Angelica outpost next door offers both savories and sweets "to go"—and since both have rabid followers, it's worth even carnivores giving Angelica a shot.

Amy Chaplin and René Durán of Angelica Kitchen

Amy Chaplin and Rene Duran may be the current keepers of the kitchen, yet the core philosophy that goes into every dish at Angelica Kitchen has remained the same for 30 years: vegan dishes using a combination of whole foods that are at least 95 percent local.

Whoever the chef or chefs at Angelica are, they play an important role in developing relationships with farmers and food artisans such as their tofu producer in Pennsylvania.

The goal is to make as much from scratch as possible, using a pantry filled with nuts, whole grains, natural sweeteners, such as agave nectar and maple syrup, and fruits and vegetable quickly after they are harvested.

"Some ingredients are eaten in 48 hours of harvesting, so the nutritional value is more intact," Chaplin says. "We make our own seitan in house twice a week as well as most of the bread. We grind nuts and oats to use as flours. The cheeses are also made in house. The only items bought premade are tofu, soy milk, rice milk and some juices."

To reflect the hot and cold seasons, the chefs change the menu twice a year, also adding in a few daily specials that highlight some of the ingredients that have shorter seasons, which they experiment with in the kitchen.

Their whimsical takes on popular everyday foods, such as quiche, croquettes and lasagna, are a hit if not always challenging.

"It sometimes frustrates me because I am trying to infuse things with lavender or whatever, but it doesn't sell as well," Chaplin says. "People really love the everyday dishes."   –Pervaiz Shallwani

AURORA RISTORANTE

Italian

510 Broome St. (W. Broadway and
Thompson St.) **1** **A** **C** **E**
212 334-9020
auroraristorante.com
Lunch 12–3:30, Sat/Sun brunch 11–4
Dinner Sun–Th 6–11, Fri/Sat 6–12

Shopping is so exhausting. Thank goodness, then—for those loaded up with H&M and Calvin Klein bags—that an excellent modern Italian trattoria is esconced in Soho. Aurora is a comfort from the moment one walks in its door. The hostess greets diners with a wide smile. Hanging tin lamps and exposed brick walls induce Old World nostalgia. The charming waiter will have a velvety, aromatic glass of biodynamic Barbera d'Alba in your hand within minutes. The wine matched beautifully with the best starter we tried—sweet coils of roasted fennel and savory homemade Berkshire pork sausage, a perfect counterpoint to mouth-puckering (and good-for-you) organic dandelion greens. The *primi* may even outshine the *secondi* here, especially a generous portion of penne mingling with hearty chunks of eggplant, grape tomatoes and luscious pieces of buffalo mozzarella that could fool an Italian grandma.

We were pleased to spy even more local sourcing in entrées: Hudson Valley-raised duck breast was rosy and crisp-skinned, and paired with a duck leg to fight over. Vegetarians and pescatarians can partake either of numerous meat-free pasta dishes or the fishy fare dotting the menu, like a moist, flaky slab of halibut tucked into parchment paper along with slices of lemon and a dusting of herbs (though we could do without the overcooked scallions served alongside them, advertised as "caramelized," but served rather burnt). That said, many gems are to be found on this menu, and we'd return in a heartbeat, particularly for the wallet-friendly pasta. One caveat: Though the atmosphere is charming—exposed pipes lend a modern edge to the otherwise rustic interior—less-than-stellar acoustics and tightly placed tables make this a late-in-the-relationship, not early, sort of date place.

It's the flagship restaurant of clog-wearing, orange-haired TV chef Mario Batali's empire. It's arguably the best-known Italian restaurant in Gotham. It is still among the hardest reservations in town to snag. And it was news to us that Molto Mario is a huge fan of sourcing local and sustainably raised fare.

BABBO RISTORANTE E ENOTECA
Italian
110 Waverly Pl.
(6th Ave. & Macdougal St.)
1 **A** **C** **E** **B** **D** **F** **V** PATH
212 777-0303
babbonyc.com
Mon-Sat 5–11:30, Sun 5–10

At Babbo, Batali's West Village eatery, push by the tourists and head to a table upstairs: The second tier of the split-level space is calm, elegant and features a skylight ringed with tiny glowing bulbs. Downstairs, though the hubbub can be a bit much, we give Babbo props for a few romantic, wide two-tops at which couples can sit side-by-side facing the room. This is the sort of place where a waiter will re-cover your tablecloth with a precisely placed napkin moments after you've dripped sauce on the table— something missing at Batali's excellent but chill little sister, Lupa (page 128)—pleasing those who like their waitstaff on the attentive side.

Antipasti, primi, secondi, contorni, and *dolce*   the staples of fine Italian fare—are all accounted for. Vegetarians can dine fairly well here, with several meat-free pasta dishes on the menu and a smattering of vegetable antipasti. Choose carefully: A platter of artichokes proved crunchy, and we wished we'd ordered the fluffy arugula salad that floated to another table. Of the pastas, we weren't crazy for organic lamb-stuffed "love letters," a signature dish, but found eggy pappardelle noodles snaking through a rich red ragú to be a worthy take on the classic. Entrées likewise impressed, especially a leggy, tender organic quail propped primly on sticks of salsify with a drizzle of *saba* (a grape *jus*). We'll return here, tourists be damned, to nosh our way through the menu—it, like the chef himself, is epic.

BABYCAKES

Vegan Bakery
248 Broome St.
(Ludlow & Orchard St.)

Ⓕ Ⓙ Ⓜ Ⓩ Ⓑ Ⓓ

212 677-5047
babycakesnyc.com
Sun/Mon 10–8, Tues–Th 10–10,
Fri/Sat 10–11

Retro chic, a Bon Jovi soundtrack, cute waitresses in jaunty 1950s style caps and sexy eyeliner—Babycakes has it all. But those who enter this LES bakery, whether celiac sufferers or vegans craving a sweets fix, will likely not notice the decor. They'll be too busy digging into gluten-free brownie bites and dairy-less cupcakes. Babycakes specializes in helping those with

allergies as well as those with dietary preferences, offering treats free from wheat, gluten, dairy, casein, refined sugar and eggs. If this laundry list of goodness has you thinking of popping in for a date, think again: only a few small stools line the walls, and the joint is cramped. But cramped in a good way—with cuteness.

As for taste, this sugar-lover was fairly impressed—the banana chocolate-chip bread here is better than the kind I snack on at the Union Square Farmer's Market—and since it's vegan, that's quite a feat. Cupcakes didn't totally float my boat, however: Babycakes whips frosting out of coconut oil, and cakes out of garbanzo flour or spelt, and my tastebuds could tell. But having sampled a few other vegan bakeries, this one is absolutely superior—and they offer cupcake tops for separate purchase, which you have to respect. So if you're starting off as a vegan or trying to moderate your sugar intake, hit that chocolate-chip bread and the brownie mini-bites—as addictive as those Whole Foods brownies that produce mania at office parties.

Savoy owner Peter Hoffman (see page 146) is the man behind this similarly locavore-friendly East Village eatery. The 2007 Oxford English Dictionary word of the year, "locavore" has come to denote "one who eats locally," a popular (and environmentally friendly) dining trend both in New York and nationwide.

BACK FORTY
Seasonal American
190 Avenue B @ 12th St.
212 388-1990
backfortynyc.com
Sun 6–10, Mon–Th 6–11, Fri/Sat 6–12

Brightly lit, with nods to the so-called "haute barnyard" movement that has stormed the city—crisp white mantles laden with china, sturdy wooden farmhouse-style tables and a simple back patio strung with bobbing lights—the restaurant serves up seasonal American fare that is almost all organic or local. So take a bite of that juicy, antibiotic-free burger covered with slabs of heritage bacon, and relax: You're eating pretty close to home here, since Hoffman sources within the tri-state region as often as possible. If you or your companions drink alcohol, several Empire State beers and wines—including an eye-opening, hoppy Bengali Tiger IPA from Brooklyn's own Sixpoint—are peppered throughout the drinks list.

Though Jared noted that there weren't many leafy greens on this menu, there were a slew of vegetable sides and several fish options. Take advantage of the fact that Hoffman's cooks know their veggies; succulent coins of summer squash were nearly candied from a spin on the grill. And although certain items on the menu were lacking—we wished grilled trout with a bland salsa verde had more kick to it—the burger alone is worth the stop-in. And having sampled the eatery for brunch, we can vouch for super savory grass-fed steak with cilantro and oregano spiked chimichurri sauce. If it's on the menu, and you eat meat, it'd be a mistake to let that one slide by uneaten.

BAR MILANO

Italian

323 Third Ave. @ 24th St. ⑥ Ⓡ Ⓦ

212 683-3035

barmilano.com

Daily 5 pm–2 am, Sat/Sun Brunch 10-3

Choose your own adventure at this Gramercy-area northern Italian eatery: To the left is a dining room distinguished by a long, charcoal-hued banquette, simple wooden tables and heavy swirled marble wall panels. To the right is the petite bar, where a special

(read: cheap!) bar menu is also enjoyed by Mario Batali, whom we spied noshing away. This was no shock, however, since his Lupa (page 128) co-owner Jason Denton is one of four partners at Bar Milano.

Happily enough, we saw intimations of Lupa here, from all sustainably raised animal products to surprisingly good pasta. A starter of buckwheat *borsetti*—coin-shaped noodles lounging in a delicate cream sauce—earned gold stars from our nutritionist, and matched well with a smooth (and biodynamic) northern Italian red wine. The "panino" appetizer was like no other we'd ever encountered: A bed of creamy polenta replaced the typical bread, and bore five ruby-hued slices of grass-fed tenderloin stacked like fallen dominoes under a dusting of spicy minced peppers. Mario and his shorts having departed, we turned our attention to entrées. Trout here is a decadent dish—a silvery fillet on tarragon-flecked smashed potatoes buttressed by two emerald stripes of scallion purée. Chicken equally impressed, in the form of an immense breast and leg spackled golden by the heat of the oven but remaining incredibly juicy, arriving plopped on a mixture of spaetzle (noodle-like curls), giblets and slightly salty broccoli rabe. But it was divine, and so massive we had to take some home. Any chicken that can make us sneak guiltily back to the fridge at midnight (a bad move, healthwise!) makes one feel downright Marioesque. Indeed, follow the way of the Clogged One when you depart, and tip in cash—your waitress (if not the IRS) will thank you.

This orange, silver and white burger chain is tricked out like an episode of *Pigs in Space* or a Stereolab album cover—modern to the max. In the Chelsea location (one of three citywide), bulbous white lights dangle from a glowing orange ceiling, and petite, shiny tables join chairs with holes punched out of them. It's a cute eatery, but since its pop soundtrack was turned up to maximum Kylie, diners won't necessarily want to linger. They should definitely stop in, however: Antibiotic-free burgers of every stripe are on offer, and they're

BETTER BURGER

Fast Food
561 Third Ave. @37th St.
4 6 6 7 5
212 949-7528
Daily 11–10:30 (Sun til 10)

178 Eighth Ave. @ 19th St. 7 5
212 989-6688
Daily 11–11 (Fri/Sat til 11:30)

587 Ninth Ave. @ 42nd St. 7 5
212 629-6622
Daily 11–10

good. And an all-natural hot dog? Better Burger, you had us at hello.

Healthy hints can be found everywhere—no surprise from the folks behind Josie's (page 123): Tap water is filtered, which is rare in a fast-food joint. Excellent all-natural condiments include a gritty but addictive stoneground mustard and a spicy homemade ketchup. Tasty "fries" are actually air-baked, and superthick smoothies—including a peppy raspberry version—are loaded with fresh fruit. As for organic beef burgers, they're juicy, piled into a wheat poppyseed bun with pickles, spirals of red onion, sliced tomato, and tough-to-find organic cheese. Dogs are free of fillers and served on whole-wheat buns. Veggie options are also on tap; we suggest noshing on a veggie burger, not the soy one—it's packed with grains and vegetables instead of less-healthy soy protein. Unfortunately, we were not impressed by the salad we tried—one of several on offer. A "Caesar" contained Romaine, sure, but also red peppers, olives, tomatoes and the strangest "Caesar" dressing we've ever tasted. Overall, we'd return: These burgers can't compete with those at Back Forty (page 83) or Hundred Acres (page 119), but for $6, they're a smart fast-food option.

BLOSSOM

Gourmet Vegan
187 Ninth Ave. (21st & 22nd St.)

Ⓐ Ⓒ Ⓔ Ⓛ

212 627-1144
Mon–Th 5–9, Fri/Sat 12–2:45/5–10:30,
Sun 12–2:45 5–9
blossomnyc.com

CAFÉ BLOSSOM

466 Columbus Ave. (82nd & 83rd)

① Ⓒ Ⓔ

212 875-2600
Mon–Fri 11–10, Sat 11–10:30, Sun 11–9
blossomcafé.com

Vegan and raw-foods restaurants sometimes have a formal, slightly sterile air: "Healthy food is on the premises!" It can be tricky to relax. This is not a problem at Blossom— particularly at its downtown location. The split-level, modern space is decked out with slim Japanese screens, ethereal curtains and pretty windowside tables, making it utterly dateworthy.

Several different regions of the world see a brief spin in the limelight, such as the American South, making a cameo in an excellently crisp cake of potatoes and black-eyed peas in a puddle of sweetly spicy chipotle aioli. An Italian tip of the hat comes via delicate ravioli floating in cashew cream flecked with sage and sautéed wild mushrooms. A Brazilian twist on tempeh finds it roasted in a savory stew of black beans spiked with orange. Avoid not-so-healthy wheat gluten (seitan) in favor of other options like two rounds of flavorful lentils, stacked and snug in a flaky phyllo crust and served on a tangle of sweet caramelized onions. Of the naturally sweetened desserts occasionally on offer, we loved a silky lavender tartlet sprinkled with über-fresh blueberries.

Uptown, Café Blossom serves a nearly identical menu with the addition of lunch offerings in a space lighter on the romance. A slim, efficient banquette wends its way down one side behind a sleek bar. Stop in for a quick bite like a tasty banana-berry shake or a hefty bowl of divinely creamy butternut squash soup. Those seeking heartier fare should stick to dinner entrées (superior on our visit to a messy hummus-and-salsa-topped veggie burger). The best were sweet potato gnocchi, served to delightful effect on a pile of jewel-toned golden and chioggia beets. Overall, we found the Blossoms a fine way to introduce naysayers to gourmet vegan cuisine at its finest.

Dan Barber's farm-to-table motif is so coyly self-aware it's almost cartoonlike. Witness the "carrots on the fence" *amuse-bouche* at his Village eatery Blue Hill, in which carrots arrive impaled on a nail-studded slab of wood and trailing long emerald fronds. Diners sit, and stare, and when Bugs Bunny does not materialize they pluck the carrots from their wires, marveling at the simple glaze of aged balsamic vinegar that causes carrot to taste, if possible, more like itself.

BLUE HILL
Seasonal American
75 Washington Pl. (6th Ave. & Washington Square Park)
① Ⓐ Ⓒ Ⓔ Ⓑ Ⓓ Ⓕ Ⓥ PATH
212 539-1776
bluehillnyc.com
Mon–Sat 5:30–11, Sun 5:30–10

The space is elegant and serene, with cushy red chairs and banquettes lining the walls, and the staff was perhaps the most charming we encountered—ideal conditions for traipsing through a menu chock-full of local, seasonal, organic ingredients. Barber helped found this trend, and his mastery of it shines both in an end-of-summer tomato salad layered with grilled peaches and swirled with ricotta, and to-die-for sweet corn ravioli. A sherry vinegar-brown butter sauce drips from bites of pasta concealing earthy pumpkin and explosively sweet corn—Indian Summer in a single bite.

Our female sommelier was a genius, expertly matching a stellar organic Spanish white wine with nearly rare sashimi-style cobia laid over a bed of crunchy macadamia nuts and diced zucchini. Even better was a plush leg of Vermont-sourced baby lamb, sitting pretty along with a smattering of buttery wild mushrooms in a wine-drenched jus. Those who must indulge in sugar might do so here: A spoonful of raspberry jam nestles inside a dark chocolate shell, arriving in a river of "milk jam"— coconut milk, milk and vanilla mingling in one sweet bite. All dairy comes straight from Barber's farm upstate, the locale of his other eatery.

Cynics might think such a wonderful place couldn't possibly be run by a down-to-earth, charming guy. We didn't think to ask when we saw him laughing with a friend before dinner, preparing to take his dog for a walk.

Dan Barber of Blue Hill

Dan Barber's philosophy toward the menu at Blue Hill is an extension of his childhood.

As a teenager, Barber was already laying the groundwork for the farm-to-table movement he has helped to bolster in the city for more than a decade.

Barber was reading about sustainability and working the fields of Blue Hill Farm in the Berkshires, developing an understanding of locally raised vegetables and animals that have extended to his own Stone Barns farm, 25 miles outside the city on the grassy hills of Tarrytown. He says he has been made into a better chef because even on his best nights of cooking, first-class ingredients trump his skill.

Barber understands the local ecosystem and uses it to his advantage. He doesn't just put meat on the menu for the sake of having meat. Instead, he understands that one of the greatest resources New England and the Hudson Valley offer is grass, the natural feed for cattle, sheep and goats.

Carrots play an important role in his cuisine throughout the year, but he showcases them in the fall, because with each subsequent frost the sugars in their roots work double-time to keep the sticks growing, adding not only sweetness (flavor), but also nutrients, like flavonoids (health).

To Barber, if it tastes good, everything else like health and environment have already been taken into account.

–Pervaiz Shallwani

Bonobo's is the sort of place a meat-eating diner expects to loathe. "Heat that nutmeat thingie up for me, wouldya?" I jauntily addressed a long-haired staffer, pointing to a drab-looking patty lurking behind the glass of the walk-up counter. The fellow gazed at me for a moment before remarking calmly, "This is a raw-foods restaurant."

BONOBO'S VEGETARIAN

Raw Vegan

18 E 23rd St. (Park Ave South & Broadway)

212 505-1200

bonobosrestaurant.com

Daily 11–8

Right you are, sir. Uncooked, vegan foods are the bread and butter (so to speak) of the airy Madison Square lunch spot, and darn them if they aren't doing a surprisingly good job. The wacky name derives from a bonobo, an ape that the Bonobo's website proclaims is "genetically most like humans," but "with no evidence of degenerative disease." Thus, their menu is packed with ape- (and human!) friendly items like nuts, seeds, vegetables and fruits. My veggie patty was not bad—like a sort of chewy veggie burger in texture and topped with a tasty, sweet sundried-tomato relish. Even more impressive were soups, which include a silky coconut-bell pepper number that would give nearby upscale Indian standby Tabla (page 151) a run for its money. As per the salad bar creations, be sure to sample before you commit; some, including bok choy with an odd sesame dressing, missed the mark. Sweets are all sugar- and gluten-free, though we haven't found any we adore yet, but the excellent housemade drinks include coconut water-sweetened piña colada, and "ginger aid": lemon, lime and ginger swirled together with agave and mineral water.

By and large, I would eat lunch here again—no small endorsement from an omnivore. My nutmeat patty and delicious soup were quite filling, and after also enjoying a savory pumpkin-nutmeat paté and crunchy flaxseed cracker, I walked out the door patting myself on the back.

BOULEY

French
120 W. Broadway (Duane &
Reade St.) ① ② ③ Ⓐ Ⓒ Ⓔ Ⓡ Ⓦ
212 964-2525
davidbouley.com
Daily Lunch 11:30–3, Dinner 5–11:30

$ $

Chef-owner David Bouley's Tribeca eatery calls to mind the chateau of a wealthy, romantically inclined French vampire: Low, barrel-vaulted ceilings curl overhead in the most seductive of deep reds; plush couches encourage leaning and lingering; dainty vintage chandeliers dangle. Bouley—the restaurant—opened in the mid-1980s, and is among the *grand-pères* of French cuisine in Manhattan. Bouley—the man—has since expanded his vision to nearby locales (Bouley Bakery and Upstairs; Secession, page 147) and will shortly move across the street and transform this space into a rendition of the Bakery.

Swing by, if you can, either way, as this is one of the prettiest spaces in the city. We were thrilled to see that the owner attends to local, organic flora (even the table settings sport pesticide-free flowers) as well as fauna (all animal products are hormone and antibiotic-free). So open the menu and pick from a prix-fixe: Even in tough times, it is clear the chef is not cutting corners, and these offerings are nothing to sniff at. Long Island duck breast was sweetly shellacked with truffles, honey and vanilla, and served with the most beautifully buttery chanterelle mushrooms we'd tasted anywhere. Even better was Connecticut farm-raised baby pig (perhaps hearkening back to the chef's own farm-boy upbringing in that state). The beast was meltingly tender, served in a savory jus and paired with crunchy sweet corn and more mushrooms—pixielike Honshimeji numbers that fairly exploded with flavor. King wild salmon on a bed of pliant jumbo asparagus was likewise quite tasty. Of the desserts that accompanied the prix-fixe menu, none were free from refined sugar, though a globe of Vermont maple ice cream came close, and was decadently creamy.

One caveat: Though this a charming space and a wonderful date spot, graceful eaves will send your cloistered conversation straight into the ears of fellow diners, so be wary.

Vegans, don't despair. There's fancy food for you, too, and not just the raw kind. This elegant Chinatown eatery has gone through a handful of chefs over the span of its short life, making critics and diners a bit wary, but when we stopped by, circa October '08, things were looking good.

The restaurant is on solid turf in the health arena; an organically inclined menu tilting vegetarian and vegan offers fish and chicken alongside tempeh and tofu.

BROADWAY EAST
American Flexitarian (Vegetarian with Chicken and Fish)
171 E. Broadway (Rutgers & Jefferson St.) (F) (J) (M) (Z) (B) (D)
212 228-3100
broadwayeast.com
Mon–Fri: Bakery 8–11:30, Lunch 11:30–3:30, Dinner 6–11
Sat: Brunch 11–4, Dinner 6–11
Sun: Brunch 11–4, Dinner 6–10

Its Green Credentials also shine: The floors of the broad space are sourced using reclaimed wood from a local water tower, and a wall of living green plants are visible from both the main space and the bar downstairs, lending indoor elegance a touch of outdoorsy authenticity and making the air as sparklingly clean as the fare. Indeed, this is a fine place for a date or a long chat with a friend—service is that unobtrusive, and long red banquettes create romantic curls for snuggling. Ask for recommendations, as gems lurk on the menu: Ravioli contained creamy faux "ricotta"—cashew cheese—and were strewn with rapini blossoms and a round, rich pomodoro sauce. A side of lotus root chips served had us obsessively dipping them in a sweet yuzu mayo, and a mélange of good-for-the-tummy pickled vegetables were among the best we'd tried. "Crispy coconut tempeh" was excellent on one visit, paired with a basmati rice cake and sweet bok choy, though less impressive in an autumnal incarnation matched with dull squash purée. Pescatarians will be pleased, however, by a plush striped bass paired with a savory purée of cauliflower and celery root. For those who tipple, the menu is full of options: All draft beer hails from the Empire State, and wines by the glass included an earthy organic pinot noir that would be easy to linger over.

CAFÉ CLUNY

French-American
284 W. 12th St.
(W. 4th & 8th Ave.)
Ⓐ Ⓒ Ⓔ Ⓛ ① ② ③ Ⓕ Ⓥ PATH
212 255-6900
cafécluny.com
Mon 8 am–11 pm, Tue–Fri 8 am–12 am,
Sat 9–4/5:30–12, Sun 9–4/5:30–11

The Village is stuffed with tasty bistros that are dimly lit and not too loud, and Café Cluny has followed in their date-friendly footsteps. In this romantic part of town, it is a comfort to find a spot where all the meat is antibiotic-free and organic, water is filtered and the produce is "either local or organic," as one waiter assured us. Though vegetarian and vegan options are scarce, omnivores should stop in, and keep an eye out for a smart prix-fixe intended to lure early birds.

The focus on whole foods is echoed by the assertive display of Nature in the decor: Botanical prints line most walls, and even the bathroom, decked out with dried flowers and the like, feels oddly comforting. Little healthy touches may be missing—here again, there were no naturally sweetened desserts, and table salt seems to be just that, not sea—but service is sweet, and swift and the fare is fine. Yellowtail sashimi was fresh as could be, sparkling with sea salt and though a little predictably paired with grapefruit, given a nice herbal touch by a sprinkle of micro-celery greens. As for entrées, a juicy, thick steak was burnished with garlic-herb butter and slim, satisfyingly crunchy fries, and was superior to ruby medallions of duck. (Note that the chef sometimes errs on the rare side here, so inquire when you order.) The bird arrived with a delicious "crepe"—an odd little igloo of dough wrapped around sweet corn and duck confit—better than the entrée. If you must splurge on desserts, order either the Ronnybrook organic ice cream indoors or—when the weather is fine—grab a cone from the restaurant cart just outside and wend through the Village streets until the last drop is gone.

Those seeking more elbow room on the perennially crowded NYC subway should take the train uptown to Café Viva, where garlic—the infamous bulb credited with everything from warding off demons to curing toothaches over the course of history—is a major player. Tucked innocuously among Broadway's banks and bodegas, this vegetarian pizzeria offers more than this immune-system booster: All the cheese is kosher and hormone-free, and bread options include unbleached white flour, whole wheat, spelt and cornmeal. Some organic produce is available, as well, like that loaded onto a top-heavy Zen slice: shiitakes, sundried tomatoes, whole bulbs of garlic, fresh pesto and green tea infused tofu. It sounds—and tastes—confusing, but it's not a bad option for vegans on the go.

CAFÉ VIVA NATURAL PIZZA

Kosher and Vegetarian Pizzeria

2578 Broadway (97th & 98th St.)

①②③

212 663-8482

Daily 11:30–11:30

$

And "on the go" is the way to dine here, instead of amid the bright burnt-orange walls and little red-and-chrome table sets. The spot is low on charm, but is a wise option for slice-cravers—especially since any sort of pie can be tailor-made. The pizza's good, though not award-winning, and includes a cheesy basic slice and an even better sauceless "Viva" on a whole-wheat crust topped with thin rounds of fresh tomatoes and nearly a handful of that fresh garlic. Skip pasta—noodles with a basic pomodoro were identical to what one can whip up at home—in favor of a side salad or a slice, and select an organic juice instead of sugary soda or ask for a glass of filtered water.

As for the garlic, it doesn't seem like owner Tony will be offering apologies for his addiction any time soon: He is so fond of the stuff that he commissioned a leggy cartoon bulb with his name on it to wave at you from behind the register while you buy your slice (wife Bella the Onion demurely bats her eyelashes).

CANDLE CAFÉ

Vegan Café
1307 Third Ave. @ 75th St. ⑥
212 472-0970
candlecafe.com
Mon–Sat 11:30–10:30, Sun 11:30–9:30

It's a good sign when you say to your waitress, "Do you have a favorite dessert?" and she replies instantly, with wide eyes, "Ohyes." Naturally sweetened desserts—delicious ones—have several hiding places in Gotham, and the Upper East Side's Candle Café is among the best: The chocolate mousse pie here would trick even a total sugar freak.

The Candle Café, the originator of nearby Candle 79 (page 95), is old school. It's been a vegetarian hotspot for fifteen years. And even at 2:30 on a Wednesday afternoon, the 3rd Avenue location remains packed with locals. Minimalist black-and-tan chairs pushed next to square wooden tables make this a casual, take-your-mom-to-lunch-and-show-her-vegan-food-is-tasty sort of place.

Indeed, the menu ranges across the vegan landscape, with smoothies (we liked a Tropical Freeze packed with mango and pineapple), salads, sandwiches, and entrées— all of it organic. Those stopping in for a drink and a snack should indulge in a satisfyingly buttery-tasting tahini-based dip for focaccia, or a hearty, tasty "Aztec" salad draped with quinoa, topped with sticks of grilled tempeh and punched up with corn, beans, a mélange of greens and a brown, nutty sauce. The three-tiered "paradise casserole"—sweet potato, black beans and millet—was decent, with an earthy gravy and a pile of slightly bitter steamed bok choy, and my tofu BLT was just okay—but if nothing else, stop in post-shopping for a slice of that chocolate mousse pie or one of their seasonal (also sugar-free!) pies. The chocolate treat is absolutely decadent; tofu and coconut oil are whipped into a silky mousse that's decidedly un-tofulike, with a crumbly, chocolatey spelt crust that tastes nothing like spelt. The whole concoction is sweetened with maple syrup. Paired with a glass of organic Riesling after dinner, I was the happiest (healthy) sweets freak around.

The posh elder sister of the chill Candle Café (see page 94) also offers a greatest-hits list of all-organic, vegan fare—tofu, tempeh, and falafel, oh, my!— to fussy Upper East Side denizens. Candle 79 is the fancier of the two, with a split-level, romantically lit interior full of plush, striped booths that encourage sprawling while dining

CANDLE 79
Gourmet Vegan
154 E. 79th St.
(Lexington & 3rd Ave.) ④ ⑤ ⑥
212 537-7179
candlecafé.com
Mon–Sat 12–3:30/5:30–10:30,
Sun 12–4 & 5–10

But stay upright long enough to select from the decent wine list, which features several biodynamic options, or tuck into luxuriously smooth guacamole, nicely showcasing the kitchen's skill with super-fresh produce or an addictive appetizer of long, rectangular blocks of lightly fried polenta. Move on to that ho-hum vegetarian standby, hummus, which gets a makeover here via red pepper-infused oil. A smoky bowl of it is served up with triangles of paratha bread, a full head of roasted garlic and a smattering of Kalamata olives. Similarly in the Mediterranean vein, a starter of hearts of palm salad mingles tiny shards of avocado with grape tomatoes and toasted pine nuts in an olive-balsamic vinaigrette. Entrées are simple but largely satisfying: Avoid the pitfalls of gluten-laden seitan in favor of, say, a cake made out of chickpeas, prettily presented, set in a drizzle of sweet coconut curry and wearing a hat of apricot chutney.

Unfortunately, the killer chocolate cake at Candle Café is not offered here, and the one naturally sweetened dessert we tried was just okay, but most treats use Florida crystals, not processed sugar—always a plus. If you must satiate that sweet tooth, housemade gingerale— pristine leaves of mint floating in a tall glass swirling with fresh ginger, bubbly with soda water, and sweetened with agave— is excellent. It's touches like these that make this classy eatery quite popular with the UES set.

CARAVAN OF DREAMS

Vegan Café
405 E. 6th St. (1st Ave. & Ave. A)
G F V L
212 254-1613
caravanofdreams.net
Daily 11–11

This assertively hippie-ish restaurant offers a kaleidoscopic array of vegan, kosher and raw foods to East Village locals and passersby. The space is long and slim, with low tin ceilings and petite tables swathed in printed, jewel-hued tablecloths. A long banquette leans up against the wall, enabling easy socializing. Though the space is slightly below street level, large multi-paned windows near the front lend it an outdoorsy glow.

For the most part, the grub here is quite good, and smoothie-cravers should definitely put it on their map; we count a couple dozen fresh juices and shakes, along with booze like sangria (too tart on one visit) and several organic wines. Chill waiters seem unconcerned if you hang out for an hour or two over a beverage and a plate of "live" raw nachos: flaxseed chips with super-smooth guacamole, bright pico de gallo and almond sour cream (excellent on one visit, decent on another). We loved a Mexican-themed platter stacked with slices of toothsome grilled tempeh, tender black beans and sweet grilled bananas on a pile of mixed veggies. On the health front, the eatery wins points for abundant organic options, more than a dozen salads on offer, the fact that sandwiches are available on sprouted whole-grain bread, and wheat-free choices like a fluffy spelt pancake served with a tiny pitcher of top-notch maple syrup. Though we weren't wowed by the naturally sweetened desserts we tried, we'll come back to keep noshing through the epic menu because the Caravan has ambiance in spades: A single mother sat down beside us, and by meal's end we knew her baby's name (Leo), her homeland (Germany), and her baby's weight (9 lbs; we ended up holding him, so she could finish her meal). Some restaurants are unconcerned about looking hippie-ish, and Caravan of Dreams, happily, is one of them.

Ah, Chipotle: The burrito chain we need not feel guilty about loving. Though recent years bore witness to a wave of panic among Chipotle-lovers, as women and men across the city panicked upon

learning that their lunchtime burrito could run them up to 1,000 calories, this chain (there are lots citywide) counts us among its fans. If you wish, tailor your burrito or "burrito bol" (Jared recommends getting bol or a salad) to be less heavy—drop the sour cream, ask for a mere sprinkling of cheese, or save half a portion for later—and rejoice in the all antibiotic-free meat, the organic cheese and the downright tasty grub. All the meats are great, particularly spicy, cumin scented *barbacoa* (beef) and tender pulled *al pastor* (pork). Indeed, even local superstar chef David Chang of pig-obsessed mini-chain Momofuku tried to get a job at Chipotle in order to find out how they make their pork, but was rejected. "They knew what I was up to," he said sadly. So swing by with fellow meat-lovers or even vegetarians: Though options are a bit more sparse for the latter, the veggie burrito bol can be strewn with green peppers and onions, black beans (caveat: the pinto beans are mixed with decidedly un-vegetarian bacon) and all sorts of fresh salsas and guacamole. The guacamole here is quite good; if you want a little more kick to yours, just spritz it with one of the free fresh lime wedges by the napkin stash. There are few fast-food chains at which to get a surprisingly healthy fix in the city, and even fewer that taste this good.

$

CHIPOTLE
Mexican, Fast Food
Daily 11–10 unless otherwise noted

100 Maiden Ln.
212 742-2690

2 Broadway
212 344-0941

200 Varick St.
646 336-6264

55 E. 8th St.
212 982-3081
Sun–Wed 11–10,
Thur–Sat 11–11

19 St. Mark's Pl.
212 529-4502

510 6th Ave.
646 336-6203

864 Broadway
212 253-7860

680 6th Ave.
212 206-3781

125 E. 23rd St.
212 673-6904

283 7th Ave.
212 645-6270

464 Park Ave. S.
212 689-0305

350 5th Ave., Ste 4–5,
@ 34th St.
212 695-0412

304 W. 34th S.
212 268-4197

9 W. 42nd St.
212 354-6760

150 E. 44th St.
212 682-9860

25 W. 45th St.
212 391-2081

620 9th Ave.
212 247-3275

129 W. 48th St.
212 575-8424

320 Park Ave.
212 754-3098
150 E. 52nd St.
212 755-9754

854 8th Ave.
212 757-4312

269 Amsterdam Ave.
212 580-6058

2843 Broadway
212 222-1712

274 Madison Ave.
212 689-1245

Like its sister restaurants—the sturdy Josephina's (page 122) and the neighborhood-y Josie's (page 123)—Citrus Grill has its own identity: Trend Central. Oddly enough for a spot on the Upper West Side, it is vaguely reminiscent of South Beach, with a spacey bright orange and white palette and silver-rimmed stools lining

CITRUS GRILL
Latin/Asian
320 Amsterdam Ave. @ 75th St.
① ② ③ Ⓑ Ⓒ
212-595-0500
citrusnyc.com
Mon–Th 5:30–11, Sat 11:30–12 am,
 Sun 11:30–11

the bar. Like its menu, the eatery is split as though by a knife down its middle. The lower level is all sleek banquettes and bright colors, whereas the second level boasts minimalist decor and a sushi bar home to stern looking chefs. This is not a subtle distinction, and the website drives it home further: "Latin Fare, Asian Flair." Okay, we get it!

Sometimes the schtick works beautifully, as in a trio of tacos— toothsome Brandt beef drizzled with tomatillo salsa, a classic pork-and-pineapple combo and chicken with a mango sauce—served with mixed greens drizzled with a sprightly miso-carrot dressing. Sometimes it doesn't, as in an ill-advised appetizer of edamame topped with overly-smoky ancho chile powder. Entrées are decent here, and include a plate of tender Long Island duck breast with a side of savory mashed sweet potatoes and haricot verts. A side of kale, meanwhile, was over-sautéed and a bit too garlicky (hopefully an anomaly). So nosh along the menu—it's certainly epic—and don't forget to sample the fruits of the sea: Silky wild salmon on brown rice was very good, and clearly fresh. Since so much is organic at these restaurants, head here for a clever mix of cuisines, to Josie's for all-organic produce and to Josephina's for a fantastic roast chicken.

CITY BAKERY
Bakery, Café
3 W. 18th St. (5th & 6th Ave.)
① ② ③ Ⓑ Ⓒ
212 366-1414
thecitybakery.com
Mon–Fri 7:30–7, Sat 7:30–6, Sun 9–5

Many of us are lured through the inviting doors of City Bakery and—not seeing the forest for the trees—halt like five-year-olds in front of the aromatic, bubbling hot chocolate machines. Though the Union Square shop's cocoa is famous for a reason, be sure to sample the often-excellent, always local and mostly organic savory fare. Not only will this cut that hit of sugar to the old bloodstream, but eco-friendly paper boxes can be filled with a myriad of savory eats to hustle over to one of several tiny, round tables in the split-level space. Hot and cold buffets feature fare that utterly defeats salad-bar stereotypes, including sprightly cilantro-flecked grilled chicken and dreamily tender roast sweet potatoes studded with golden pineapple cubes. Even soups and stews are a success, including a ratatouille so richly aromatic it would cut through a head cold. Several salads are always on offer, and I couldn't get enough of a lentil number—and I am no lentil proponent, I assure you—proving that the Bakery does well by tough-to-love items, too. (Listen up, people with kids!) So if you need to trick little Jimmy into some greens alongside his cocoa, this might just be the place to do it.

Those stopping in for brunch will be just as pleased; organic eggs come strewn with red pepper and shards of green onion, and an excellent French toast is crackly like a crème brûlée and served alongside organic, top-grade maple syrup. This is part of many foodie tours of the city, and popular with locals—witness the cute couples huddling over those tiny tables, and the women meeting for a chat—though the hubbub downstairs can be deafening weekends and weeknights, so plan your visit carefully.

That the proprietors of longtime downtown fave Clinton Street Baking Company are still succeeding at comfort fare—now across town, in Morningside Heights—will come as no surprise to those who wait in long lines for their burgers and brunch. Happily, the newer eatery has not only a different menu, but a greater focus

COMMUNITY FOOD AND JUICE

Seasonal American

2893 Broadway (112th & 113th St.)

212 665-2800

communityrestaurant.com

Mon–Fri 8–3:30/6–11,
Sat 9–3:30/6–11, Sun 9–3:30/6–10

on organic fare. We snagged seats on the sidewalk under the luminous, gawk-worthy lanterns, but suspect we would have been just as happy inside, esconced on a long banquette facing the slim, industrial space. Tall ceilings and floor-to-ceiling windows do a fine job letting the light shine in, and exposed piping gives an aura of an art gallery-cum-eatery.

Health-friendly options abound, starting with the beverages: Water is filtered, and there are a dozen organic or sustainable vino options for those who tipple. And vegetables prance happily across the menu, from a local tomato salad dotted with homemade ricotta to a jewel-hued, tender "bowl of beets" married to sweet goat cheese, to the substantial, choose-your-own-veggie sides alongside the fish and meat of the day. Of these, you'll have to pick and choose to find the best: We weren't thrilled by undercooked Brussels sprouts that came alongside a juicy organic strip steak topped with a melting slab of herb-spiked butter. The fish of the day did better, arriving plump and tender atop a tumble of sautéed onions and mushrooms in a pool of Thai red curry sauce to swipe them through. Among ample vegetarian options are the rice bowl—a simple mix of brown rice, prettily julienned carrots and cukes, bean sprouts and bright bits of cilantro and mint, with a sesame-lime dressing to tie the whole together. Mercifully, you can even end this meal feeling good: The eatery is certified by the Green Restaurant Association for its environmentally sound practices, from composting to energy-efficient kitchen equipment.

COOKSHOP
Seasonal American
156 10th Ave. @ 20th St. **C** **E**
212 924-4440
cookshopny.com
Mon–Fri 8–11/11:30–3/5:30–11:30
Sat 11–3/5:30–11:30, Sun 11–3/5:30–10

Looking at art while gallivanting around Chelsea is hunger-inducing, so thank goodness for places like Cookshop, where the fabulous people brunch. Every table in the clean, high-ceilinged eatery—it resembles a gallery in layout—seemed to be occupied with a moneyed arty type or

L.A. transplant. In short, this is where Chelsea denizens (and their friends) brunch. Occasional tourists seem to be acceptable, as long as they look good.

The fare was solid, with a few standouts: Though we were disappointed by the refined sugar on the table and the fact that not all produce was organic, husband-wife owner team Vicki Freeman and Marc Meyer (see Hundred Acres, page 119, and Five Points, page 110) pride themselves on sourcing locally, and it shows. For one, a giant chalkboard in the back of the restaurant features a diagram of a cow's edible parts—thank goodness the chef does well by the mooing stuff. The tender beef brisket we dove into was carved from cows raised on an eco-friendly farm in Virginia: Bits of sweet caramelized onions floated alongside punchy bits of red pepper, with the whites of two perfectly poached eggs making a ghostly trail atop the whole. Less impressive was the buzzed-about Cookshop Scramble: Though it's worth sampling for those organic eggs, the taste of applewood bacon was muted, as was the crème fraîche supposedly mixed in. Opt, instead, for antibiotic-free chicken salad. Thick slabs of the bird come on a giant pile of mixed greens spruced up with green olives, golden raisins and a splash of tart, Mediterranean-inspired vinaigrette. Sea salt is on every table, we noted, so one can sprinkle a few crystals on anything lacking. Happily, at Cookshop, not much is, including the people-watching. As we left, a woman preened on the outdoor patio, sunning herself in a hat that looked to have been vertically sliced in half—an ode to Picasso, perhaps? Ah, Chelsea.

Those who have wandered the East Village late at night, whether after a few drinks or after emerging from the cinema on Second Avenue, probably had no idea that a burrito joint—an organic burrito joint—hovered in their mist, like a UFO above Midwestern plains.

COSMIC CANTINA

Mexican, Fast Food
101 3rd Ave. @ 13th St.
4 5 6 N Q R W L
212 420-0975
Daily 12 pm–5 am

Forgive the simile, but the Cosmic Cantina inspires otherworldly comparisons. It's organic, cheap and pretty darn tasty compared with neighboring grease-slingers. And with $3.30 organic beers like Peak Organic Nut Brown on offer, it's likely I'll never darken the doorway of San Loco or Benny's Burritos again. Note that the Cantina is not a date place; it's a spot to grab sangria, a pitcher of suds or a bunch of burritos with friends. The pop or punk music inside is often at full tilt and the tables are strange, towering X-shape numbers with stools perched precariously around them, but the sidewalk area, dotted with wicker seats, is pretty cozy for a summer or fall afternoon. The place gets hopping in the evening, so either order your burrito—we loved the oregano-spiked, olive oil-sautéed mélange of zucchini, squash and red pepper on offer for vegetarians—"to go" or have some patience with your riotous neighbors: NYU kids and the like come out here in droves. Tuck into a tasty antibiotic-free chicken burrito stuffed with black beans (tastier than pintos), a spelt-wrapped veggie burrito or a duo of tacos topped with a bright pico de gallo. Avoid lemonade—a honey-sweetened beverage sounds good in theory, but in practice is like guzzling straight honey water—and stick to H_2O, organic juices or organic brews. Nothing's going to break the bank, and you'll feel better about yourself as you head out into a rollicking night in the Village (or into that cab).

COUNTER
Gourmet Vegetarian, Bar
105 1st Ave. (6th & 7th St.)
6 F V L
212 982-5870
counternyc.com
Mon–Th 5 pm–12 am, Fri 5 pm–1 am,
Sat 11 am–1 am, Sun 11 am–12 am

Counter: What the heck is it? East Village passersby may be pardoned for this thought while trotting by the dark-but-upscale cave of a vegetarian restaurant on an odd little stretch of First Avenue. Thankfully, the otherwise dim restaurant has a glass façade that opens cleanly onto a sunny street, ideal for watching aging punk-rock women sporting brightly hued spectacles trot by. The space is quite pretty, and focuses on the letter O: It dangles in a design from bronze strands in the doorway, comprises the meaty, metallic base of the short, inviting bar and decks out the bathroom. We reckon O must stand for "organic," since everything here is, and the food—we swung by for brunch—was more impressive than anticipated.

Start with coffee, if you drink it; it's excellent here, and although agave was not available, the natural sweetener stevia was. Sangria, for those who wish to indulge, is strong and dense, featuring sweet red wine, orange juice and the muscle of brandy. And not a single entrée failed us: Delicious spelt French toast tasted nothing like its namesake, helped along by a spin in the frying pan and a drizzle of decadent flambéed bananas. Silky walnut-lentil paste "paté" was another hit, among the best we sampled anywhere, here spread generously on foccacia with rosemary aioli and plum tomato—a cute twist on a French classic. Even an all-organic-egg frittata was tasty, though the portion size was a bit meager, and a side order of sautéed escarole struck that lovely none-too-garlicky note. Counter prides itself on its fancy cocktails—much ado was made of the "world's hottest cocktail" when they put the pepper-spiked elixir on their menu—and judging by that sangria, it could be good. But the food is what left our mouths in Os, so swing on by.

Deborah Gavito of Counter

Deborah Gavito had been working part-time doing paste-up work at *The Village Voice* and selling vegan pastries in the Green Market when she got the idea for Counter: a vegetarian restaurant that does nothing more than blend in with the urban chic culinary jungle of New York. What she has honed since 2003 is a style of vegetarian that focuses on the experience as an integral part of the food.

She fostered socially responsible drinks by creating an extensive bar with organic, biodynamic and sustainable wines, spirits and beers. "I wanted the restaurant to be accessible to everyone and having a bar helps," she says.

Gavito built a restaurant that is curvy, colorful and inviting, a place people want to be because it leads by example, not a place that preaches to them. "I wanted it to be welcoming to non-vegetarians. It should be an example," Gavito says.

And finally, she settled on Mediterranean cuisine because it is healthy and diverse, showcasing vegetables, legumes and healthier fats like olive oil instead of butter. "Probably 70 percent of our customers are not vegetarian, maybe even more. Our customers are pretty educated. They choose to come here. They are not your average, poor-eating American. They are health conscious and progressive."

Along with the socially responsible alcohol, Counter's menu offers a series of choices: organic grains and vegetables when available, homemade over store-bought ingredients such as tempeh and seitan, natural sugar over refined (except for simple syrup and raw sugar for coffee because she finds natural sweeteners just don't work).

"It's a whole lifestyle," Gavito says. "You are not only doing something good for your body, you are supporting sustainable agriculture and taking care of the environment."   –Pervaiz Shallwani

CRAFTSTEAK
Steakhouse
85 10th Ave. @ 15th St.
212 400-6699
craftrestaurant.com
Mon–Th 5:30–10, Fri/Sat 5:30–11
Sun 5–9

$ $
$ $

We're not going to lie to you: We love steak. We prefer it organic, and are even more smitten when it's grass-fed, so we were over the moon to find a Chelsea steakhouse with sustainably raised, all-organic cuts of beef. Kudos go to owner (and *Top Chef* judge) Tom Colicchio of the Craft restaurant empire, whose menu touches upon most every type of beef, from Wagyu tartare to a grass-fed ribeye. What we sampled, happily, was delicious.

The toffee-and-gold hued space is precisely between a nightclub and a restaurant, ambiance-wise, with stratospherically high ceilings, skinny modern light fixtures and curling, intimate banquettes. Waiters so skilled they might be invisible deliver piping-hot bread sparkling with sea salt—or an *amuse-bouche* of über-earthy chicken liver mousse with tummy-friendly homemade pickles—before you've even cracked the menu. (Since none of the wines by the glass were biodynamic or organic, we stuck to filtered water.) Though each meat came with a note about its home, none were from New York, so we jumped at a striped bass that was. Paired with a starter of a sprightly arugula salad laced with thin rounds of fennel, the flaky fish will please most pescatarians. As per sides, local sweet potato fingerlings were so naturally sweet they tasted like candy, and sautéed Swiss chard was among the best we sampled anywhere. Oh, and that steak. The chef briefly sears it and tosses it in the oven, keeping it juicy. Our grass-fed ribeye had a nice crust, was tender as could be and served with four possible partners: Horseradish-spiked crème fraiche and a thin, herbaceous chimichurri sauce didn't float our boat, but béarnaise sauce laced with tarragon proved an excellent foil to the savory, aged-on-the-premises meat. Final touches included one of the few naturally sweetened desserts we've seen at a high-end eatery—a honey-sweetened orb of local organic ice cream. Top notch, Top Chef.

Only in New York can you snag an order "to go" from a tiny, nondescript fried chicken joint and realize—probably after sinking your teeth into a crisp-skinned, slow-roasted rotisserie bird or an astoundingly juicy fried drumstick—that this is grub from a haute cuisine veteran and a James Beard Award (the Oscars of food) winner. Co-owner Allison Vines-Rushing has worked with renowned international restaurateur Alain Ducasse, and although you wouldn't think a simple bite of bird would reveal her vast skills, you'd be wrong.

DIRTY BIRD TO-GO
Chicken, Fast Food
204 W. 14th St. (7th & 8th Ave.)
① ② ③ Ⓐ Ⓒ Ⓔ Ⓕ Ⓥ Ⓛ PATH
212 620-4836
dirtybirdtogo.com
Daily 11–10

The fare Vines-Rushing and her husband are turning out in a tiny to go spot just north of the West Village is, believe it or not, good for you. Of course, rotisserie chicken is a healthier choice than the crispy stuff (which is soaked in buttermilk and fried in peanut oil), but every Dirty Bird sent out the door is hormone- and antibiotic-free and locally raised. And if you have to go for the fried stuff, the oil they use for frying is recycled for biodiesel fuel. Sin with a side of sautéed garlic kale—it's excellent here, dotted with chile peppers and garlic—instead of the few drab iceberg salad numbers. Take note: The joint means it when it calls itself "to-go"; seats are few and far between. But swing by with a friend who doesn't mind the hubbub of a largely takeout operation, and enjoy the not-at-all-dirty birds.

ELETTARIA

Indian, Eclectic
33 W. 8th St. @ Macdougal St.
1 A C E B D F V PATH
212 677-3833
elettarianyc.com
Sun/Mon 5:30–11, Tu–Sat 5:30–11:30

Though Elettaria is tucked onto a skinny strip of the West Village better known for touristy t-shirt shops and shoe stores, we heartily recommend it not only for fine fare—organic produce and grass-fed and organic meats ranging from duck to pork—but the luxe, gorgeous interior that makes it an ideal date spot. The space is well-designed, with a heavy emphasis on seductive lighting, exposed brick and heavy red velvet drapes that help partition it into both a posh bar area and an open kitchen in the back for those who wish to gawk as their meals are assembled. The tiny tables are knee-knockingly close, but not uncomfortable. Chef Akhtar Nawab, a veteran of the Craft mini-empire, specializes in South Asian fare, and prioritizes sourcing organic meats and produce. Jared was pleased to note a number of healthy spices dotting the menu, and we both found the eats to be top-notch. Though there weren't oodles of options for vegans and vegetarians (there was a lone dosa crepe entrée and a few veggie-based starters), this is a place for conscientious meat-eaters. A crab meat resala came across like a deconstructed crab cake: Succulent, tender morsels of the meat came in a pile surrounded by tiny globes of fried batter and drizzled with a sweet turmeric soubise. Jared was a fan of the tender grilled steak, and I loved the plush, salty strands of king oyster mushrooms that surrounded it. Though we didn't sample dessert—none were sugar-free—we noted a few organic wines on the list. I will return here to perch on one of Elettaria's cushiony bar stools, nosh my way through the rest of the menu and sip a glass of sweet Empire State-made Riesling.

Adjacent to Madison Square Park lurks another member of Danny Meyer's Gotham entourage, perhaps the most beautiful of any, with Art Deco touches, including trapezoidal copper wall sconces and a minimalist leaf outline adorning soaring walls. Admire them from an enormously comfortable high-backed chair, a chocolate-colored leather banquette or the petite but elegant bar.

ELEVEN MADISON PARK

Contemporary American
11 Madison Ave. @ 24th St.
Ⓡ Ⓕ Ⓥ Ⓡ Ⓦ
212 889-0905
elevenmadisonpark.com
Mon–Th 12–2/5:30–9:30,
Fri 12–2/5:30–10, Sat 5:30–10

Chef Daniel Humm has earned acclaim on a national level, and as Eleven Madison's prices may indicate, he does not mess around. Nearly every meat is certified organic, and local touches such as Lynnhaven Farm goat cheese tucked into tortellini and served in a minestrone emulsion—a foam of pesto and tomato—are par for the course. Humm's menu—New American inflected with the foams and gels of molecular gastronomy—will please daring diners. But he also succeeds with the basics: A mâche salad was wreathed with frisée and dotted with melt-in-your-mouth halves of quail eggs and bits of salty bacon. For entrées, we looked to our waitress for help pairing a vino (this wine menu won the 2008 James Beard Award for excellence). Unfortunately, the organic Gewürztraminer she suggested was too sweet to contrast well with delicate arctic char paired with petite rounds of squash and Brussels sprouts ("petite" is the operative word; those who want their vegetables should snag a salad). Succulent beef tenderloin was the star main course, crusted in bone marrow and served with braised oxtail and Swiss chard. The meat was beautifully marbled, and the oxtail was divine. The only thing missing, in our opinion, was a sugarless dessert, so consider this our plea for the pastry chef to join Mr. Humm in his laboratory to concoct a treat using agave, maple or honey. For now, a über-professional waitstaff delivers the sweet send-offs.

FIVE POINTS

Seasonal American

31 Great Jones St. (Lafayette St. & Bowery) ⑥ ⑧ ⑩ ⑥ ⑥ ⑥ ⑩

212 253-5700

fivepointsrestaurant.com

Mon–Fri 12–3/5:30–11:30

Sat 11:30-3/5:30-11:30

Sun 11:30-3/5:30-10

This flagship of the Marc Meyer/Vicki Freeman triumvirate (Hundred Acres, page 119; Cookshop, page 102) was established in 1999 and remains a champion of locally procured goods and organic animal products. The pan-American eatery is more sizable than its sisters: To walk in is to immediately note its high ceilings and long bar teeming

with patrons clamoring for a glass of wine or a unique cocktail (lime-and-lavender gimlet, anyone?). Keep going and take a gander at that "fountain" slimly lining the room; it's a hollowed-out oak tree.

The fare here is likewise solid and hearty—bistro food with a kick. Line-caught Alaskan salmon may not be regional (it is FedExed in each morning), but it was perhaps the best we sampled. The flesh was rosy and luscious, and served atop a summery ragout of pigeon peas, green beans, corn and sparkly mint. We couldn't get enough of it. Pair it with a starter of wild arugula and goat cheese salad dressed with a simple roast shallot and olive oil vinaigrette—we dropped our forks swearing we'd not eat anything else for the duration of the summer. Carnivores can tuck into a grass-fed burger topped with fat, lazy slabs of smoked bacon, so juicy it required extra napkins. The sole disappointment was pasta: An entrée portion of house-made cavatelli mingling with bacon, roast corn and chives lacked kick. But this airy, elegant space deserves another visit; the service was smart, adeptly pairing a not-too-sweet Riesling with our salmon. (Though there were no organic or local vinos by the glass, draft beers included local suds-makers Sixpoint and Captain Lawrence.) Next time we might reserve the large, pretty table lit by a skylight in the back of the restaurant—ideal for a celebratory dinner out.

"Eat. Think. Be Organic," read the brown t-shirts of the workers at this Rockefeller Center area lunch spot. Indeed, it's a clean place to eat clean food, and perhaps the brightest with natural light of any we surveyed. Floor-to-ceiling windows illuminate comfy, Jetsons-like brown-and-white swivel stools at the eatery, which features an impressive salad bar, a number of raw foods, and many vegetarian and vegan items.

FREE FOODS
Café
18 W. 45th St. (5th & 6th Ave)
① ② ③ ⑤ ④ ⑤ ⑥ ⑦ Ⓝ Ⓠ Ⓡ Ⓦ
Ⓐ Ⓒ Ⓔ Ⓑ Ⓓ Ⓥ
212 302-7195
freefoodsnyc.com
Mon–Th 7:30–8, Fri 7:30–4:30

Matthew Kenney, an original owner of Pure Food and Wine (page 137), is the man behind the eats here—soups, salads and hot entrées—and although it costs a couple dollars more than at nearby eateries, all the grub is organic, and yes, you can taste it. Both soups we tried—a decadent lobster bisque and a vegan soup that somehow mustered a creamy zucchini/split-pea base that was not too "vegetable-y"—impressed us, as did a made-to-order salad with a tangy gingery dressing, crunchy chickpeas and sprightly baby arugula. Pre-prepared offerings varied a little more in quality: Salmon flecked with mango was a touch overcooked, and a terrine of tomato sauce, raw tomatoes, pesto and nut cheese was just... so...tomato-y. Nor did I love our bland tofu sandwich. That said, a charming level of eavesdropping is the name of the game here, and long raised shared tables almost seem to encourage flirting among the cleancut midtown types. Jared was pleased to see a few vegan desserts, including a few containing organic sugar, though he would have preferred to see agave used. Most important, Free Foods takes its nature schtick seriously. Not only do blades of grass and bright blue skies line the posted menus, but all cutlery and cupware is biodegradable.

GILT AT THE NEW YORK PALACE HOTEL

Eclectic
455 Madison Ave. @ 50th St.

Ⓔ Ⓔ Ⓔ Ⓔ Ⓕ Ⓥ

212 891-8100
giltnewyork.com
Fri–Sat 5:30–10:30, Tu–Th 5:30–10

"Opulent" is the only way to describe this restaurant esconced in The New York Palace Hotel. Gawk at the glittering chandeliers in the foyer. Dance up the luxe carpet-covered steps, like Annie on her first day at Daddy Warbucks' house. Enter the magical eatery itself, passing through a bar decked out with a giant golden sci-fi-esque sculpture and into a human-size jewel box. High carved mahogany ceilings soar overhead; cushy corner tables curl into dateworthy two-tops; wall sconces lend intimate lighting. With seamless service to boot, no wonder Gilt makes "most romantic" restaurant lists year after year.

Thankfully, chef Christopher Lee—whose artlike, eclectic cuisine nods to the molecular gastronomy movement—is down-to-earth, healthwise. Water here is filtered, and the menu is laden with organic animal products and produce. Most every creation is breathtaking: Silky, ruby-hued slices of Tasmanian sea trout find ideal foils in clouds of foamy white yuzu and a swath of spicy wasabi-soybean cream. We also loved a plate resembling a Russian avant garde painting: A long red rectangle (Jersey cranberries) sits under a globe of squash, next to a foam of ricotta sprinkled with nutmeg, several more drops of squash purée and a tangle of mustard greens. Entrées continued in this visually arresting pattern. Seven pale slices of Peking duck encrusted in pecans lay on a river of bright, sweet huckleberry jus next to a stripe of bright-orange sweet potato purée. Ever-so-tender lamb loin came with a vegetable backup band of a few Brussels sprouts, thin rounds of fig and a bit of kale. As for desserts, though none are naturally sweetened, the prix-fixe mandates one—snag a fruit plate if you wish to avoid sugar or look for dessert like a pretty crème brûlée sprinkled with tropical fruits. Request the check, and the waiter just smiles, instead delivering a final sweet touch of coconut-pineapple soup. The Gilt life, it seems, should not be rushed.

As the heavy, forbidding wooden doors that grace its entryway suggest, this eatery offers Serious Vegetarian Fare. Even the notoriously veggie-blind food press has paid the restaurant (and its uptown sibling) notice, with a review in the "$25 and Under" section of *The New York Times*. Gobo's atmosphere is reminiscent of an upscale sushi restaurant embedded in a posh salon: Cushioned banquettes line the walls and three elegant, boxy lighting fixtures illuminate the stretch of the main hallway. At night, the joint is jumping, but at lunchtime your companions might include only a few quiet businessmen sipping sweet pineapple iced teas. And although service was a little scattered, our dishes came flying out of the kitchen.

We'd have to agree with the paper of record's assessment that the fare is a bit hit-or-miss. But when it hits, it hits hard. Pick among the menu and be sure to avoid the processed soy products—they're everywhere, and they're not good for you—and instead select a tasty starter like lightly fried scallion pancakes topped with a pyramid of sweet mango salsa or a packed-with-minerals seaweed, kale and beet salad. Soups seem to be among the kitchen's forte; a calming, wintry number came with a broth so savory it resembled chicken broth, with a few root vegetables and tender white beans lazing about. Of the entrées, try an autumnal faux-lasagna—sweet potatoes layered with rice "pasta" and kale was a quite convincing incarnation of the classic, though it might not fool your Italian cousin—rather than a gummy green beans-and-eggplant creation, which had been over-sautéed. Though no desserts are sugar-free, a vast selection of fruit-packed, sugar-free smoothies are available, and tipplers can peruse an impressive list of wine and beers that include several organics, putting the cap on the notion that this is fine vegetarian dining, indeed.

GOBO
Eclectic Vegetarian
401 6th Ave. (Waverly Pl. & 8th St.)
① Ⓐ Ⓒ Ⓔ Ⓑ Ⓓ Ⓕ Ⓥ PATH
212 255-3902
goborestaurant.com
Daily 11:30–10:30

1426 3rd Ave. (81st St.) ④ ⑤ ⑥
212 288-4686
Daily 12–10:30

GOTHAM BAR & GRILL

Contemporary American, Eclectic
12 E 12th St. (University & 5th Ave.)
① ② ③ ④ ⑤ ⑥ Ⓝ Ⓠ Ⓡ Ⓦ Ⓕ Ⓥ Ⓛ
PATH
212 620-4020
gothambarandgrill.com
Mon–Th 12–2:15/5:30–10,
Fri 12–2:15/5:30–11, Sat 5–11, Sun 5–10

Alfred Portale's eatery has earned many accolades over the years, most recently from *New York Magazine* critic Gael Greene, who called it one of the 14 most important restaurants of the last 40 years. We didn't think the eclectic, pan-European fare could stand up to such acclaim, but it did, from start to finish.

We swung by the airy Union Square eatery at lunch, and our gazes floated instantly upward to the inverted jellyfish-like fabric light fixtures looming overhead (perhaps a nod to the vertically plated food Portale is famous for). Although we wished filtered water and organic wines by the glass were on offer, and that more vegetables accompanied entrées, we otherwise loved a fairly priced prix-fixe, including such gems as a robustly creamy soup looped with pretty rounds of sweet Vidalia onion and an organic yellow beet and mango salad featuring giant cubes of the fruit and vegetable interspersed with baby arugula, shaved fennel and sweet microbasil.

Vegetarians can certainly find treasures here, particularly on the à la carte menu, which features the best wild mushroom risotto I've ever tasted. The grains of rice were melt-in-the-mouth tender, and the dish is amplified tableside by a mushroom emulsion that foams and spits as it coats a mélange of petite mushrooms that look plucked from Snow White's film set. Grilled organic New York strip steak also wooed us— cumin-encrusted rounds of meat lazing in a seductively savory streak of wine-inflected *bordelaise* sauce. Even roast haddock gets a makeover, served in a lemon foam that wreathes parsnips, leeks and a silky potato purée. All in all, and with flawless service, this Gotham-within-Gotham is a very true execution of the city's high-end culinary spirit.

This member of Danny Meyer's coterie (including Tabla, page 151; Eleven Madison Park, page 109) occupies a sedate stretch just north of shopper-packed Union Square. The eatery has received renewed attention since chef Michael Anthony took the helm in 2007, and with a focus on knowing its farmers, ensuring sustainable use of animals, and local, mostly organic produce, it deserves it.

GRAMERCY TAVERN

Seasonal American
42 E 20th St. (Park Ave. South & Broadway) ④ ⑤ ⑥ Ⓝ Ⓠ Ⓡ Ⓦ Ⓛ
212 477-0777
gramercytavern.com
Tavern: Sun-Th 12-11,
Fri/Sat 12-12
Main Dining: Lunch Mon-Fri 12-2
Dinner Fri/Sat 5:30-11 Sun-Th 5:30-10

Two restaurants essentially cohabit one awning: Up front is a casual tavern featuring broad, blowsy murals of cabbages and onions, and a long, wooden bar. Profusions of flowers in the foyer call to mind an elegant potpourri shop, and the more formal dining room features Impressionist-era portraits, so this is definitely where we'll bring Mom when she's in town.

Anthony's fare is less outré than Eleven Madison Park's, and solidly American. Excellent (and obscure) brews like Maine's Allagash Black are on draft, as were two organic reds by the glass, including a velvety Côtes du Rhône. This matched well with a delicious starter of merguez (all meats are antibiotic free)—thin tubes of delicately spicy lamb floating in a supersavory broth, along with fresh chickpeas and split almonds. Also impressive was a silky, good-for-the-liver Jerusalem artichoke soup drizzled with beads of orange juice. Another appetizer—heirloom cauliflower—glowed royally purple, flaunting its vitamin-packed nature under a flurry of golden raisins and crunchy almonds. As per entrées, we were underwhelmed by undercooked chicken, but excited by grass-fed roast beef generously stuffed into foccacia and paired with a über-salubrious dandelion salad. The dandelion greens were the best we'd had anywhere, dressed simply in a creamy lemon dressing to temper their sharpness. Though no naturally sweetened desserts are to be found, sweet farewells from the charming hostess will follow you out the door—yet another reason Mom will love it.

Michael Anthony of Gramercy Tavern

As the executive chef at Gramercy Tavern, Michael Anthony is the most recent steward of one of the city's most celebrated farm-to-table restaurants. The alumni include a long line of legendary chefs: Tom Colicchio (Craft), Marco Canora (Hearth), Jonathan Benno (Per Se).

Each chef has left his own mark, and since 2006, Anthony is no different, developing relationships with farmers and showcasing their food on the menus in the restaurant and the more relaxed adjacent tavern, where the food is more rustic.

"It's all a balancing act," he says. "It's not an easy concept to define. We look to make contacts with suppliers who are roughly in a day's drive and working hands on and closely with the food."

Under Anthony, the kitchen has undergone a physical reorganization, developing space to butcher entire animals instead of using only certain cuts. For Anthony, it's an important part of the ecological cycle.

"All of these things are linked. We have come to realize that having animals on farms is a cycle. The restaurants follow suit. We have to be part of that cycle. It's all connected."

It has helped him to execute his philosophy, which emphasizes using everything an ingredient has to offer whether it's using the scattering of a pig across the menu or an entire Swiss chard, the leaves used to make a sauté or salad, the stems sliced into batons, pickled and used as a tangy garnish.

"It's a much more interesting way to eat," he says. "I think one of the main things that defines the way we cook. I think health and enjoyment go hand-in-hand."   –Pervaiz Shallwani

NYC's Chelsea Market is admittedly a strange dining destination. The former Nabisco factory looms forbiddingly over several Chelsea blocks, evoking a sort of gothic hobbitville for adults. Traipse down an echoing, industrial hallway, where every crumbling, falling-apart brick-covered arch reveals a new artisanal food

GREEN TABLE @ CHELSEA MARKET

Seasonal American
75 9th Ave. @ 15th St.
① ② ③ Ⓐ Ⓒ Ⓔ Ⓕ Ⓥ Ⓛ
212 741-6623
cleaverco.com
Mon–Sat 12 pm–10, Sun 11–5

purveyor such as beloved local Amy's Breads or antibiotic-free ice cream vendor Ronnybrook Farms. But among the best discoveries here is the heartbreakingly tasty burger at The Green Table.

It was so quiet and cramped at the few, bare-bones tables inside the tiny orange-walled space that we felt more comfortable at a communal table facing the mechanized "waterfall" in the main hallway. There, we eyeballed a slim menu touting "fresh, seasonal, local, handcrafted" American classics. Almost all of the mostly organic food was a success. Our burger was made of Empire State-raised, grass-fed beef and Flying Pigs Farm pork, and arrived plump on a roll from Amy's. Sweet tomato relish is lavished on top, along with couldn't-believe-it kimchi and the crispiest bacon we've tasted in ages. The result is a sweet/tart/salty combo that had us declaring this one of the best burgers we'd found. Not quite as thrilling was a grilled cheese; supposedly made with raw-milk cheddar, herb butter and apricot compote, we could taste only the cheese. Better was a substantial side salad of frisée tumbled with bright slices of orange. Bird-lovers, don't despair: There's a great free-range chicken potpie on offer here. Break the shiny, crackly pâte brisée crust to reveal moist slices of dark meat, corn and peas in a savory broth. It's available "to go" from the fridge, and given the spare seating and slightly forgetful service, we wouldn't blame you if you snagged a pie or that burger and kept going.

HANGAWI
Korean Vegetarian
12 E. 32nd St.
(5th and Madison Ave.)
Ⓖ Ⓑ Ⓓ Ⓕ Ⓥ Ⓝ Ⓠ Ⓡ Ⓦ
212 213-0077
hangawirestaurant.com
Mon-Fri 12–3/5–10:30,
Sat 12–3/3–10:30,
Sun 12–10 (dinner menu only)

If there's a more calm-inducing restaurant lurking near chaotic, shop-infested Herald Square, we haven't found it. This dreamlike Korean eatery comes with only one caveat: Be prepared to lose the shoes. A line of them marks the foyer, so kick 'em off, step up onto clean wooden boards, tread to your seat, and slip below-ground—or so it feels—to sit on slim cushions at a low table. Though this may sound high-maintenance, the zenlike effect of the space—glowing orange walls, modern low-lit lighting fixtures, ornate Korean art—is that of an upscale yoga studio.

The all-vegan fare possesses equally sedative properties: A slim all-organic menu comes tucked into a "regular" menu. Among its wide-ranging offerings were a delicious dandelion and avocado salad with a peanuty wasabi sauce in which nutty dressing and buttery fruit nicely counter the bite of super-salubrious dandelion greens. We stuck to this menu as much as possible, and were equally impressed by its entrées. Mushrooms (present in most dishes) are scattered liberally through a brown rice-and-onion mixture served in a hot stone bowl. Bits of rice darken as they press up against the side of the bowl, so snag the proffered hot sauce to swirl through the whole, let it all keep cooking, and midway through your meal, start breaking crunchy bits off the side—they're addictive. Steamboat soup is—par for the course—pacifying: Clean, thin and aromatic as all get-out, slim oyster mushrooms contribute a woodsy flavor to the veggie-spiked broth. Tea here—fresh ginger strips floating in a giant mug with honey and a wedge of lemon—is unmissable. So get a pedicure, skip yoga and head to Hangawi. Just try not to nap. By meal's end Jared and I were both sprawling with eyes half-open, propping ourselves up against the wall—a rare happenstance in Gotham.

This newest member of the Cookshop/ Five Points trifecta boasts an identical husband-wife owner team and the same desire to source locally. The trendy West Village eatery also sports a see-and-be-seen bar area, with a dining room up front made slightly noisy by pretty white tiles lining the bar. Japanese-inspired lanterns hang overhead, French windows open to the street and a general sociable buzz dominates—the back room or petite garden might be better for a sedate evening out.

HUNDRED ACRES
Seasonal American
38 Macdougal St.
(Prince & Houston St.) ① C E R W
212 475-7500
hundredacresnyc.com
Mon-Fri 12–12, Sat 11 am–12 am,
Sun 11–4/6–10

I have dined here once before, and happily, the food has undergone a 360, with all the entrées and most of the appetizers impressing us both. Jared delighted in options for what he terms "healthy omnivores"—organic chicken, grass-fed beef, myriad fish and a selection of vegetables for those who don't eat meat (though veggie entrées were sadly lacking). Health-friendly sea salt graced the table, but happily, none of the food—whether a sweet slice of bluefish perched atop garlicky eggplant purée or a grilled pork chop matched with spicy peach "catsup"—required it. In fact, our fries were quite over-salted, but the staff quickly replaced them with those to our taste. Beet greens, of huge nutritional value, also made an appearance, and their dark leaves were toothsome and buttery.

Service, too, has much improved. Our bartender ably paired a Malbec—many wines here are organic or biodynamic—with a decadent chicken liver mousse. And as per burgers, this may be the time to add cheese. All-natural Pennsylvania-produced aged Goot Essa cheddar added a slightly earthy note to a downright juicy grass-fed burger. One caveat: A treviso-and-blackberry salad comprises eight slices of naturally tart treviso under an even more bitter berry dressing. So although the occasional misstep remains at Hundred Acres, by and large, the kitchen has gotten it together.

IL BUCO

Italian
47 Bond St. (Bowery and Lafayette St.)

212 533-1932
ilbuco.com
Sun 5–11, Mon 6–12, Tu–Th 12–4/6–12,
Fri/Sat 12–4/6–1am

An out-of-towner calls and demands a proper introduction to New York dining—someplace "chic, European and very New York." Take him to Il Buco. The Italian eatery is almost dauntingly Old World, imbuing the throwaway adjectives "beautiful," "rustic" and "romantic" with real meaning via a visual cacophony of hanging copper pots, dark wooden antiques, profusions of flowers and whimsical metal light fixtures. We braced ourselves, for surely chef Ignacio Mattos couldn't compete with this level of charm. But he did, starting with knockout starters: A huge square of lasagna concealed spicy organic beef, kale and heady, gorgeous taleggio amidst its folds. Vegetable "carpaccio" of razor-thin zucchini and squash equally impressed, with a jolt of citrus juice, sparkles of mint and curls of salty parmesan. Perusing the menu while waiting for entrées, we noticed the restaurant's use of local purveyors, listed on its back like a starting lineup. Foodies and locavores alike will be impressed to see heavy hitters like upstate's Flying Pig Farm (bacon) and Ronnybrook Farms (milk). As per health, Il Buco gets high marks for sea salt, filtered water and organic animal products—though we wouldn't have minded seeing more dark greens on offer, especially with such hearty meats. Pork belly was extremely fatty (as is its wont), so trust the waitress when she emphasizes this or prepare to fill up on its sides of snappily fresh peas and soft white beans. Fish proved a better option that evening—a fillet of hake delivered lightly fried, crisp, and alongside a gorgeous array of heirloom red and yellow tomatoes for a bite of acidity. This is absolutely a date place, but call ahead and be sure you get your own table; it may be European to sit at a loud, jovial, communal table, but in the glow of candlelight, it's preferable to dine with just one other.

If monks lived in the East Village and needed a chill place to sip a microbrew and nosh on a locally sourced snack, they would head here. The hobbithole-like gastropub features vaulted ceilings, arched doorways and a cloistered, abbey-like feel. Located just below street level on a chill strip of East 7th Street, the heavy wooden furniture and slightly hushed atmosphere make it a surprisingly romantic watering hole, especially early in the evening.

JIMMY'S NO. 43
Bar, Seasonal American
43 E. 7th St. (2nd and 3rd Ave.)
Ⓖ Ⓡ Ⓦ Ⓕ Ⓥ
212 982-3006
jimmysno43.com
Sun–Th 12 pm–2 am,
Fri–Sat 12 pm–4 am

Owner Jimmy Carbone is a major proponent of sourcing locally and organically whenever possible, and even earned the Slow Food Snail of Approval for his food's "quality, authenticity and sustainability." Not bad for a bar. Jimmy's has two things in spades: high-quality, mostly local and organic fare, and microbrews. So if you're going to drink beer, this is the place to do it. All-natural and local options are abundant, including Brooklyn's Sixpoint—I sampled one of their tasty, hoppy IPAs—and wonderful upstate New York brewery Captain Lawrence. As for international options, Jimmy suggests all-natural German beers as being among the friendliest to pair with food, which have none of the candied sugar that a Belgian ale like Chimay delivers.

Though celebrated chef Phillip Kirschen-Clark had departed as of August 2008, the interim cook had everything on his menu under control when we stopped by: Non-gamey medallions of lamb came drizzled with an addictive mint-yogurt sauce, and an heirloom tomato salad was among the best we sampled, with bright disks of tomato resting on a pillow of sweet, locally made ricotta and mozzarella di bufala. Overdone burger sliders were less impressive, but a farro salad speckled with radicchio and curls of preserved lemon was sprightly, and a nice nod to vegetarians. All in all, the monks have it good at Jimmy's.

JOSEPHINA
American
1900 Broadway (63rd & 64th St.)
1 A C B D
212 799-1000
josephinanyc.com
Sun 11–11, Mon–Fri 11:30 am–12 am,
Sat 11 am-12 am

The folks are in town, they want to see a show at Lincoln Center, and it's up to you to make dinner reservations. You procrastinated, and now everything is packed or incredibly pricey—and who wants to make mom and pop pay an arm and a leg for dinner?

Thankfully, there's Josephina, a sedate but tasty, parent-friendly restaurant directly across the way from the performing arts center. Brought to you from the same folks behind organic-focused Josie's (page 123), Better Burger (page 85) and the Citrus Grill (page 99), organic meats, mostly local and organic produce and charming service are all on offer here, and often at the last minute. Just be sure to book a table in the front room, with its giant, faux-Renaissance era mural, rather than the black-and-white tiled, back room that looks more like a deli, or a clattering extension of the kitchen itself.

This is the sort of place where entrées are so ginormous one might almost get away with simply ordering entrées. "Pan-crisped natural chicken," for example, was modestly advertised, but arrived with a splash, as slab upon slab of juicy bird fairly climbed out of the bowl it arrived in. The breasts had been pan-seared, with a dark shellac and an appealing crispness, and accompanied a tasty corn cake. Also lovely were tender, ruby-hued medallions of organic filet mignon, seared to black on the outside, and sharing a plate with a savory medley of sautéed asparagus and wild mushrooms. Fish offerings were more disappointing: A starter of crab cakes were pummeled with red pepper bits, and a striped bass special served with bok choy proved similarly unexciting (though we fought over creamy truffled potatoes that accompanied it). Waiters here are clearly accustomed to folks hustling to make a curtain: From soup to nuts, we dined under an hour, but didn't feel remotely rushed. This is an accomplishment in the oh-so-busy Upper West Side, to be sure.

With tentacles —healthy ones!— stretching across the city's dining scene, this Upper West Side outpost of the Josie's/ Josephina (page 122)/ Citrus Grill (page 99)/ Better Burger (page 85) mini-empire occupies the medium-fancy end of the dining continuum, with tubular, sparkly lights providing refracted ambiance along the span of floor-to-ceiling windows and sunny yellow walls. Pan-American eats are intended for vegetarians and carnivores alike, with a menu featuring mostly organic produce, all antibiotic-free meats and an emphasis on sourcing locally. We squeezed in and found that—though this isn't a date place, the

JOSIE'S
Seasonal American
300 Amsterdam Ave. @ 74th St.
① ② ③ ⑧ ⓒ
212 769-1212
josiesnyc.com
Mon–Th 12 pm–11 pm, Fri 12–12, Sat 11:30–12, Sun 11–10:30

566 3rd Ave. (37th St.) ④ ⑤ ⑥ ⑦ Ⓢ
212 490-1558
Mon–Th 12 pm–10:30 pm, Fri/Sat 12–11, Sun 12–10

1614 2nd Ave. (84th St.) ④ ⑤ ⑥
212 734-6644
Daily 5:30–10

service is a bit wonky and the neighboring conversations can be loud—it's obviously a neighborhood place, if the stream of chattering customers is any indication. They come for the food as well as the fine wine list, which included a number of sustainable and organic vinos. I went with a swell rosé crémant—a sparkling French wine—and was not disappointed.

We liked, but didn't love our meal: The best thing we tried was a starter of pan-seared black bean dumplings in a sweet mango sauce, though pumpkin soup drizzled with pesto was a fine nod to the leaves falling outside. Organic chicken was not quite as tasty as it was at sibling Josephina, but it certainly had size on its side: A giant breast and thigh dwarfed the plate, and accompanied prettily julienned carrots and zucchini. Plump pieces of grass-fed strip steak proved fairly tasty served with lightly sautéed bok choy, and a tuna burger was lent oomph by wasabi mayo and pickled ginger. Skip optional sides of dull smashed potatoes and instead tuck into (more healthful) air-baked fries or sweet potatoes. We would have loved to end on a sweet note, but found that—though wheat- and dairy-free options were on tap—none were naturally sweetened. We'll cross our fingers that Josie will add this to her epic menu.

LE MIU
Japanese & Sushi
107 Avenue A (6th & 7th St.) Ⓛ
212 473-3100
lemiusushi.com
Sun–Wed 5:30 pm–12 am,
Th–Sat 5:30 pm–1 am

After searching high and low for sushi establishments featuring all antibiotic-free meats and eggs, Jared was pleased to discover this slim, welcoming restaurant in the East Village. Dull track lighting lines the ceiling and ho-hum exposed brick line the wall, but the tableware is pretty, and the space is elegant compared to its oft-Spartan competitors. Most important, the food is quite good.

Since Le Miu's menu is light in vegetables, perhaps start with a mineral-rich salad towering with four glistening varieties of seaweed, a fresh green salad drizzled with truffle oil or a bowl of warming red miso soup. Entrées were tempting across the board, particularly pork ramen; since a boom in late 2007, the East Village has become the heart of ramen country. The bowl here is generously proportioned, with giant, tender slices of pork and oodles of noodles, but it's not the best in the neighborhood. It might be a good way to initiate the unsuspecting into a ramen-crazed state matching your own, though, before dragging them off to an all-ramen joint. So what's unmissable? Creatures of the sea—particularly an excellent lobster ceviche. A globe of peach sorbet melted onto buttery pieces of the crustacean sprinkled with bright black roe. In a nod to bigshot Nobu's signature dish, miso-marinated black cod is also on offer here, lushly tender and served with piles of carrots. For sushi and sashimi, look to your environmentally friendly guide (see page 54) and perhaps select mackerel, which we ordered *hako*, or "Osaka-style," clean and elegant with the fish pressed into a square shape alongside rice, shiso (an aromatic member of the basil family) and biting ginger. Though there are no organic wines and the water's not filtered here, the sometimes-great food—I've had dreams about that ceviche—and focus on organic options would entice us back in a flash.

This U.S. outpost of a Belgian chain—the name is French for "daily bread"—does well by our health standards and just squeaks

LE PAIN QUOTIDIEN
Café
Multiple Locations (see next page)

by in the taste department. We find ourselves charmed both by the philosophy of coming together over one great table (a feature of the original as well as its seventeen New York area siblings) and the clean, airy, European like decor of light wooden tables and chairs.

Le Pain's large menu encompasses brunch and lunch alike, including vegan soups, organic breads (Jared loves that spelt, in addition to wheat and white, is available), eggs, tartines (essentially open-faced sandwiches) and salads. Diners will need to sample among the menu: A dry turkey sandwich was a bit lacking, as was an oomphless, rather too-oceanic seaweed salad. But an excellent quiche with a thick crust was loaded up with organic eggs, spinach and just a touch of Gruyère, and arrived with a sizable array of vegetables: tossed salad, a wedge of bright melon and several thick slices of tomato drizzled with pesto. Coffee is organic and brought to the table with organic milk and, if you want it, agave (hard to come by in this town!). Try to snag a regular coffee mug, though; the shop offers what we'll call "faux lait" bowls that open widely at the top and lack handles. It looks cute, but the wide surface area means a cold bowl of coffee. But a charming waitress offered a free pot when we mentioned this, so we hope they'll change to mugs across the board. Regardless, a cup of joe paired with a sizable bowl of very good steel-cut oatmeal topped with a flurry of bright berries is a fine way to start a day of shopping (Loehmann's is right across from the Chelsea location—just saying) or sightseeing.

LE PAIN QUOTIDIEN
Café
Mon–Fri 7:30 am–7:30 pm, Sat/Sun 8 am–7:30 pm unless otherwise noted

1270 1st Ave.
(68th & 69th St.)
212 988-5001
Mon–Fri 7 am–7:30 pm,
Sat/Sun 7:30 am–7:30 pm

1131 Madison Ave.
(84th & 85th St.)
212 327-4900

252 E 77th St.
(2nd & 3rd St.)
212 249-8600

833 Lexington Ave.
(64th & 65th St.)
212 755-5810
Mon–Fri 7 am–7:30 pm,
Sat/Sun 8 am–7:30 pm

50 W 72nd St.
(Columbus Circle &
Central Park West)
212 712-9700

494 Amsterdam Ave.
@ 84th St.
212 877-1200

60 W 65th St.
@ Columbus Ave.
212 721-4001
Mon–Fri 7:30 am–8:30
pm, Sat 8 am–8:30 pm,
Sat/Sun 8 am–8 pm

2463 Broadway @ 91st St.
212 769-8879

922 7th Ave. @ 58th St.
212 757-0775
Daily 7 am–8:30 pm

70 W 40th St.
(5th & 6th Ave.)
212 354-5224
Mon–Fri 7 am–7:30 pm,
Sat/Sun 8 am–7:30 pm

550 Hudson St.
@ Perry St.
212 255-2275
Mon–Fri 7 am–7:30 pm,
Sat/Sun 8 am–7:30 pm

38th E 19th St.
(Broadway & 5th Ave.)
212 673-7900

124 7th Ave.
(17th & 18th St.)
212 255-2777

100 Grand St.
(Greene & Mercer St.)
212 625-9009

81 W Broadway
@ Warren St.
646 652-8186
Mon–Fri 7 am–7:30 pm,
Sat/Sun 8 am–7:30 pm

801 Broadway @ 11th St.
212 677-5277
Mon–Fri 7:30 am–8:30
pm, Sat/Sun 8 am–8:30
pm

10 5th Ave. @ 8th St.
212 253-2324

Take it at its word and go liquid at this petite East Village smoothie shop and juicery. The joint specializes in organic, vitamin-spiked fruit-and-vegetable concoctions, and although most sandwiches are not worth the investment—a veggie burger was

LIQUITERIA
Juice Bar, Café
170 2nd Ave. @ 11th St. 6 R W L
212 358-0300
liquiteria.com
Daily 8 am–10 pm

unremarkable; tuna proved bland—the juices are downright delectable. Swing by before a movie or after a shopping outing (and just swing by; this is not a place to camp out). The small space is almost entirely open-air, for one thing; floor-to-ceiling glass panels vanish in warm weather, and most of the half-dozen tall orange stools are full on weekends. Small benches out front are lovely for watching the punk passersby and sipping a papaya paradise, packed with a mélange of tropical fruits like banana and papaya and a hit of none-too-overpowering coconut. Service here has improved since the early years, when one could wait for an order for what seemed like hours: Now, it's prompt and friendly. I loved the premade "grasshopper"—a pale green elixir of apple, pear, wheatgrass and mint—given such a supersweet kick from fresh pineapple juice that I had one of those "I can't believe it's not sugar" moments. Our nutritionist notes that the best-for-you juices are, oddly, in the actual refrigerated compartment at the front of the shop, and not made on the spot. Evidently Liquiteria uses a cold press extraction method that preserves the nutrients of the fruit.

Raw foodists will be happy to note a small selection of snacks, but taste-wise, we were happiest with those liquids. I can safely say that—instead of a wintertime cocoa or summertime milkshake—that grasshopper might be alighting in my purse next time I'm in the East Village. High praise indeed from a self-professed sweet tooth.

LUPA

Italian
170 Thompson St.
(Houston & Bleecker St.)
212 982-5089
luparestaurant.com
Daily 12–12

"Italian food is comforting" is a ubiquitous truism, but in a town full of glitzy eateries, jam-packed vino-by-the-glass bars, and subpar red sauce joints, it can be tricky to pinpoint a heart-warming Italian trattoria. Happily, there's Lupa. The West Village restaurant co-owned by Mario Batali has been churning out excellent Old World fare for many years. Don't let its hubbub dissuade you from eating there. Make a reservation or arrive early as a walk-in; you can always linger at the bar to admire the exposed brick interior and European feel of the place over a glass of vino selected from the extensive wine list.

To cut the wait, consider the long wooden communal table by the front: There's plenty of elbow room, and a chance to ask a neighbor about those beets drizzled with cream sauce and speckled with pistachios (they're worth it) or the roast summer squash aromatic with thyme and mint (even better). Save plenty of room for Lupa's buzzed-about pasta. The famous gnocchi was, on this one visit, stuffed with sausage and fennel, and it was good, but we enjoyed the basic pomodoro (tomato sauce) spaghetti even more. Batali's classic onion, carrot and thyme base makes for a surprisingly sweet sauce, and gets a spicy edge from chili pepper flakes. As for entrées, though fish is fine—skate was pleasantly buttery, and served with fried caper berries—we liked the (all antibiotic-free) meat the best. Pork shoulder was prepared using autumnal herbs like clove and nutmeg, but not to potpourri-like cloyingness; its deep-brown skin was crunchy, sweet and addictive, and the meat itself unbelievably moist. Small coins of steak arrived beautifully rosy, with a charred, dark ring, and were tender as could be—which is how we felt about Lupa after our meal.

Buoyantly friendly service, organic bottles of wine around the twenty-four dollar mark, and Asian-inflected fare are the unexpected hallmarks of this Upper West Side restaurant. A neighborhood standby, the largely vegetarian eatery seems almost to have been airdropped from the East Village.

MANA

Asian, Macrobiotic
646 Amsterdam Ave. (91st & 92nd St.)
① ② ③
212 787-1110
manaorganic.com
Daily 11:30–10

But no matter: The grub is good, the water filtered, and for health-conscious locals, the mostly organic menu is a gem of a discovery.

Ignore the slightly spartan decor—plain wooden tables strewn haphazardly around the room—and focus on the food. An aromatic miso-based vegetable soup delivers a hearty autumnal oomph via a few skinny wood ear mushrooms and *okonomoyaki*—our cheery waiter laughed as we struggled to pronounce it—a savory Japanese buckwheat pancake, is delicately fried up and served with sweet sundried tomato sauce. Pescatarians will delight in a number of fish options: Six crop up on the menu. We quite liked the frequent special of wild cod, flaky and moist, and served with a simple tamari-and-ginger glaze and a side of creamed millet. Though it may not sound crave-worthy, the millet will please polenta-lovers; the golden, smooth grain resembles that Italian staple in taste, and is the consistency of creamy mashed potatoes. But perhaps the best part of dining here are the many vegetable options: Bok choy and broccoli sautéed with ginger and garlic may sound run-of-the-mill, but it has a crispness and freshness that calls to mind a jaunt through the garden. As for the sugar-free desserts, none wowed us completely, though a fruit crisp dessert was decent. As you clear your plate, look around the spic-and-span joint, let the owner know how you liked the fare (she often tours the room to ask each diner) and note that she is cleaning the tables herself. It's just that sort of place.

MAS FARMHOUSE
French
39 Downing St. (Bedford & Varick St.)
①ⒶⒸⒺⒷⒹⒻⓋ PATH
212 255-1790
masfarmhouse.com
Daily 6–11:30

This willfully cloistered restaurant is in the West Village, a part of town that by its very topography feels top-secret, as high heels echo on quiet cobblestone streets. Push open the heavy wooden door to find an elegant, low-ceilinged homage to a French farmhouse ("Mas" is the Provençal word for it). Though

we haven't yet seen a farmhouse with such an elegant bar space—five leather-covered stools, a cozy sitting area—and such pristinely white tablecloth-covered tables in the small formal dining area, we're sure there's such a thing somewhere.

The largely organic menu sources very close to home, which should please locavores, and seasonally changing fare is at its best brilliant and at worst, still quite good. Caveat emptor: The eaves of this "farmhouse" hang low, so ask for the corner table or compete with your neighbors for conversational rights. The chef offers two prix-fixe tastings, and—judging by the slightly finer cuts of meat in the identical dishes we ordered landing on the table next to us—it's possible he prefers preparing these. Even if you select à la carte, note that chef Galen Zamarra, who trained in France, does beautifully by seafood: His starter of basil sorbet, shredded crab and a tomato-water consommé tasted like—well, like falling in love. The sorbet melted effortlessly into the consommé bath, adding a tint of sweetness, and pale strands of crab were tender as could be. A starter of tuna tartare was seared to rare and covered with curls of salty crispy shallots, and an entrée of striped bass arrived with punchy, sweet corn. The sole disappointment was the duck, which we had to saw through—never a good sign. So go fishing, as it were, try not to eavesdrop on the stock-trading habits of fellow diners, and note that the staff has surreptitiously put The Who on the stereo. This farmhouse, it seems, is open to all of us.

If you don't want to break the bank before that Lincoln Center play or Central Park ramble, put Nanoosh on your radar. The humble chickpea is the focus of this hummus-centric eatery, with the beige bean making a starring appearance in two boxy, dangling glass light fixtures as well as all across the menu. Nanoosh,

NANOOSH
Mediterranean Hummus Bar
2012 Broadway (68th & 69th St.)
① ② ③ Ⓑ Ⓒ
212 362-7922
nanoosh.com
Daily 11 -10

its slogan boasts, has been offering "fresh, organic, natural" fare to the neighborhood for a year , and as we went to press, was expanding to a new UES Manhattan location. Most, though not all, of the produce is organic, and all of the meat is antibiotic-free.

Hummus here is for those who like a super-tahini edge and almost peanut-butter like consistency to the classic Mediterranean dish. Though clearly very freshly made, it's very thick, and not always my bag— I preferred the version topped with spicy, crumbled beef that, along with a few toasted pine nuts, effectively cut its density. Even better were wraps, particularly chicken—lean strips of the bird tucked into a thin, handmade wheat wrapper and speckled with organic onions, greens and tahini. Salads were a bit hit or miss. An über-healthy quinoa salad was packed with juicy raisins and bits of pepper, and available for only $3.50 as a side. But the Nanoosh green salad is almost 70% carrots—no joke when they say it's grated on top—and we found little relief from the tart arugula in either of the citrus dressings offered. But Jared was pleased to see digestion-aiding mint in my delicious, brown sugar-sweetened lemonade, and I was happy to see that several varieties of popular organic ale Peak's on offer. Perhaps the best aspect of Nanoosh—a fine discovery for those who left their picnic planning to the last minute—is that they deliver to Central Park. Hummus on demand: Gotta love New York.

NATURAL GOURMET INSTITUTE

Culinary School
48 W. 21st St., 2nd Floor
(5th & 6th St.) Ⓕ Ⓥ Ⓡ Ⓦ PATH
866-580-1801 ext. 0
naturalgourmetschool.com
Fri Night Vegetarian Dinner ($40 inc.
tax; reservation required) 6:30–8:30

What if you could visit the chefs behind the Angelica Kitchens, Blossoms, and Pure Food and Wines of the future? At the Natural Gourmet Institute's "Friday Night Dinners," you can, and walk away full, to boot.

The Institute has been offering vegetarian-focused chef training for pros and amateurs since 1977. Once a week, their midtown space transforms into an ad-hoc restaurant. Menus are strictly vegan and organic, the modest prix-fixe includes tip and tax, and drinkers can BYO wine or beer. Though metal folding chairs, long communal tables and slightly odd table decor—fake leaves and gourds, anyone?—may leave those accustomed to fancy dining turning up their noses, that just leaves more room for the rest of us.

A five-course meal is served up by what can only be called a bevy of servers, often relaying plates to one another as though sandbagging a dam. Since food may travel the course of the room before making its way to your mouth, the multi-hour meals are not for the impatient. Was it worth it? Absolutely. Spinach and white beans "two ways" included a tasty soup "shooter" of spinach, and wonderfully flaky strudel pastry came wrapped around bean purée and more spinach. A second course of mixed greens and juicy pomegranate seeds also boasted five tender roasted Brussels sprouts. The veggie-packed mania continued into the excellent main course, with a prettily presented risotto "cake." Sauteed chopped kale, Arborio rice, mushroom and sage pesto were stacked atop one another in a pool of sweet butternut squash purée. A trio of naturally sweetened tartlets with a cinnamon-vanilla steamer (almond and rice milks) were a little less exciting, though we liked one of cranberry and a touch of dark chocolate in a tiny oat flour shell. At the end, pepper the students with questions, if you wish—like truly classy chefs, they emerge to greet their guests.

Whether it's Ethan Hawke perched on the steps of a café or John Leguizamo emerging from the chill environs of One Lucky Duck toting a Bunny Brew—a raw juice loaded with carrot, apple and ginger—Irving Place is becoming known for its celeb sightings. And if you pick an oddball time—we hit Takeaway at 2:30 on a weekday and snagged a small table amid the colorful pillows—the odds of great people-watching tilt in your favor.

ONE LUCKY DUCK

Raw Café, Juice Bar
126 E. 17th St. (Irving & 3rd Ave.)
④ ⑤ ⑥ Ⓛ Ⓝ Ⓠ Ⓡ Ⓦ
212 477-7151
purefoodandwine.com
Daily 10–11

At this tiny outpost of beloved neighboring Pure Food and Wine (page 137), all the raw, vegan fare is concocted below 118 degrees, satisfying purists, and many goods are gluten- and nut-free. Savory food proved very tasty; tortilla wraps were malleable and tender, unlike at many similar restaurants, and topped with a sweet sundried tomato spread, smooth cashew cream and a sprightly citrus-tinged guacamole. This, paired with a towering sea vegetable salad of wakame, arame and beets, had us full for hours. Of the freshly extracted juices—the eatery boasts a Norwalk Hydraulic Press juicer, which allows for minimal oxidization of healthy nutrients—we liked the "Thai Green," a savory elixir loaded with pineapple, cilantro and lime. A mango-raspberry smoothie likewise had that eye-opening freshness one expects when paying what are admittedly slightly high prices. But if there's one thing worth paying a premium for here, it's sweets: Pure Food and Wine puts almost every other restaurant we sampled to shame with its naturally-sweetened treats. A faux-mallomar comprised of a pillow of cashew cream, a sprinkle of cocoa and a nutty, earthy base would trick any sugar hound, and a chocolate ganache tart was smoothly, effortlessly decadent. Though I might skip an overly cashew-y take on an Oreo, I'll be back for that mallomar. The sugar-free life never tasted so good.

ORGANIQUE

Deli, Café
110 E. 23rd St. (Lexington Ave. &
Park Ave. South) ⑥ ⑧ ⑩
212 674-2229
organiqueonline.com
Mon–Fri 7:30 am–9:30 pm,
Sat 8:30 am–7:30 pm,
Sun 10:30 am–7:30 pm

Of the multitude of midtown delis, it's pretty swell to find one that— amid the chemical-filled, fly-dotted buffet bars—offers clean, organic produce and meats for only a dollar or two more. Organique is one such place. The slim space is set up like a typical New York deli, though it seems less crowded than most. Modern decor includes a handful of white plastic tables and a few chairs lining the walls, and it's a fine place to pick up lunch "to go" or an organic cup of joe in the morning.

True to its name, Organique boasts organic produce whenever possible—and labels those items on three large menus that hover over the salad bar. Of the all-organic meats, we quite liked the turkey, moist slabs of which were available by the pound, and wild salmon flecked with dill. (Get there on the early end of the lunch rush—the fish tends to dry out on the heated buffet tins!) Skip not-so-fresh sushi and slightly dry burgers and instead take advantage of the salad bar, with dressings like agave-sweetened miso, or some of the delicious roast vegetable options, which seem to be the kitchen's forte. Baked canoes of deep-orange sweet potatoes came dotted with plump cranberries, and a twist on ratatouille, a mélange of roast eggplant and tomatoes, was melt-in-your-mouth tasty and a nice homage to the late summer season. So though we noted a few places to improve (only iodized salt was available), we were also pleased by touches like filtered water, organic milk for coffee and the locally made 5 Boroughs ice cream available up front. Though it won't be winning awards for Best Manhattan Deli any time soon, choosing smartly among the menu items can yield some surprisingly tasty results, and is a smarter choice than similarly priced neighboring fast-food joints.

This simple, organic and locally focused soup and sandwich chain is an English import, and it ably contradicts any lingering misapprehensions about the caliber of that country's food.

PRET A MANGER
Café, Fast Food
Multiple Locations (see next page)

Instead of potato-based or greasy fare, the charming shops—typically chock full of tiny tables, a few maroon banquettes, and feather-printed wallpaper—proffer sandwiches, soups, cakes, cookies, muffins, juice and coffees. The 42nd Street location, one of over a dozen citywide, is usually packed with Gothamites seeking a slim, tea-style sandwich stuffed with plush avocado and organic Bell & Evans chicken, or one of several usually tasty soups, like a luscious seasonal puréed butternut squash number. Salads here are often a success, especially a tender salmon and green bean version.

Pret—as the locals call it for short—also succeeds in the beverage arena. Fair-trade, organic coffee is very good, and since beans are rotated (and composted) every two weeks, that cup of joe has an especially fresh kick to it—hard to find in midtown in the morning! The organic milk offered alongside is a swell bonus. If you require something cooler to sip, snag a green tea sweetened with mango or any one of a few sugar-free smoothies. At the 42nd Street location, Bryant Park is just across the street, and makes for a fine place to unwind over one of these elixirs or a sweet blueberry-and-pomegranate yogurt drink

Though tiny healthy touches—sea salt instead of iodized salt, for example—are still missing, this is a fine eatery to snag a quick lunch to go or to stay. Everything's made fresh daily, and leftover sandwiches are donated to charity. This, alongside the fact that most food containers are biodegradable as possible, will make most diners feel good about their meal as they head back to work.

PRET A MANGER
Café, Fast Food
Mon–Fri 7 am–7 pm
(call for weekend hours)

60 Broad St.
(Beaver & Exchange St.)
212 825-8825

530 7th Ave,
(38th & 39th St.)
212 825-8825

287 Madison Ave.
(40th & 41st St.)
212.867.0400

1350 6th Ave.
(on 55th St. btw. 5th &
6th St.)
212 307-6100

630 Lexington Ave.
@ 54th St.
646 497-0510

11 W 42nd St.
(5th & 6th Ave.)
212 997-5520

30 Rockefeller Center,
Concourse Level
212 246-6944

135 W 50th St.
(6th & 7th Ave.)
212 489-6458

205 E 42nd Street
(2nd & 3rd Ave.)
212 867-1905

400 Park Ave.
(54th & 55th St.)
212 207-4101

380 Lexington Ave.
@ 41st St.
212 871-6274

1410 Broadway @ 39th St.
646 572-0490

425 Madison Ave.
(48th & 49th St.)
646 537-0020

1200 6th Ave.
(on 47th St. btw. 47th &
48th St.)
646 537-0030

485 Lexington Ave.
@ 46th St.
646 688-1052

1020 6th Ave. @ 38th St.
646 688-1061

757 3rd Ave. @ 47th St.
646 688-1050

708 3rd Ave.
(44th & 45th St.)
646 810-2425

880 3rd Ave.
(53rd & 54th St.)
646 810-2422

There's no other way to say it: Pure Food and Wine sexes up raw food. With its red velvet seats, made-for-seduction low lighting, and a romantic garden a nattily-dressed older gentleman one table over described as "to die for," owner Sarma McIngailis's posh Union Square area restaurant is a tribute to gussied-up, uncooked food.

PURE FOOD AND WINE
Gourmet Raw Vegan
54 Irving Pl. (17th & 18th St.)
④ ⑤ ⑥ Ⓛ Ⓝ Ⓠ Ⓡ Ⓦ
212 477-1010
purefoodandwine.com
Daily 5:30–11

This doesn't mean that for two folks largely accustomed to seeing their food—well, cooked—a noodle-less lasagna isn't going to be a bit of a shock. But the setting makes it all go down easy, and we were impressed by a few inventive twists on classics. Of the starters, a seasonal salad of watermelon—two thick bars of the rosy fruit sandwiching a tangle of baby arugula, a scatter shot dose of toasted pistachios and a punch of coarse pepper—impressed with over-the-top freshness. Less successful was a faux-ravioli appetizer; limp "noodles" stuffed with cashew filling tasted vaguely peanut-buttery. The kitchen finds its stride in the entrées. Lasagna comprised of thin slices of zucchini, a sweet sundried tomato sauce and a persuasively creamy pine nut cheese was tasty and pretty, to boot. A main course of zucchini blossoms stuffed with cashew cheese in a possum-like imitation of mozzarella, arrived on a bright bed of soft avocado pyramids and sparklingly fresh grape tomatoes.

Please do not skip dessert: It's mandatory to order whatever dairy-free ice cream is on offer, whether it's cardamon-lime, in which the intense herb is beautifully mellowed, or a brilliant, towering V of an ice cream sundae, packed with globes of bright mint ice cream and logs of dense, toothsome chocolate. All ice cream is naturally sweetened and dairy-free, and boy is it brilliant. So snag a glass of organic or biodynamic wine, and hang out in that garden with a friend over that sundae. There are worse ways to spend an evening.

Sarma Melngailis of Pure Food and Wine

There is nothing militant about Sarma Melngailis' approach to raw food.

It started as a two-week experiment to see what eating raw was like and became a lifestyle of roughly six years.

She did feel better, but what she noticed was that most people eating raw had no idea how to make it "lovely and appealing" to the mainstream.

At Pure Food and Wine, Melngailis takes her traditional culinary training and combines it with raw principles (no processed or refined foods, no meat and cooking nothing over 117 degrees) to create high-end, restaurant-quality food using the best local and organic ingredients.

What she has created is a restaurant that appeals to everyone, but happens to be friendly to eaters with vegetarian, vegan or raw food diets.

"We are trying to make it something that people can integrate into their lives. Most of our regulars are not raw food people at all."

She loathes fake, processed meats such as seitan or tofu. She and her staff — many of whom come from some of the best restaurants in the city and rarely have a background in raw food — take whimsical approaches to classic dishes, using mushrooms to create their own take on meaty sushi rolls or creamed cashews to hand-craft aged cheeses.

She has applied the same principles to her popular desserts, avoiding impurities with soft coconut in place of cream, and agave nectar for refined sugar, to guarantee not skimping on taste.

–Pervaiz Shallwani

Many of us are under the impression that wheat pasta is always going to be second-best—that it's one of those compromises we must force ourselves to like. For my part, I'd always put down a fork-swirled bite complaining about the excessive wheatiness of the noodle.

I saw the light, however, in the fairytale-esque garden of Quartino Bottega Organica, an unassuming

QUARTINO BOTTEGA ORGANICA

Italian, Vegetarian
11 Bleecker St. (Bowery & Lafayette St.) ⑥ Ⓑ Ⓓ Ⓕ Ⓥ
212 529-5133
Mon–Wed 12–11, Th–Sat 12–11:30, Sun 11–10
Cash only

little Bleecker Street eatery. Here, the whole-wheat, organic pasta is made on the premises and served with, on one occasion, meltingly tender baby artichoke hearts and a dusting of parmigiano reggiano. And if there's a better way to recover from a grueling day of Nolita shopping, I'm not sure what that might be. In addition to said pasta, the menu also has several vegan options. Though we didn't adore our "risotto"—brown rice flecked with basil and tomato—we quite liked gnocchi in a simple, sweet tomato-basil sauce. Pescatarians, take heed: There's no beef or chicken here, but there is always a fish of the day, simply treated (usually grilled or baked). The menu is trim but well curated: foccacia, wheat pizza, veggie sides like an excellent baked spinach, and—this had our nutritionist smiling—a brunch menu chock-full of local organic eggs, which can be hard to come by in this part of town. Wine drinkers should know that there are plenty of organic vinos available. With an interior decked out with copper accents and pretty, dim round lights, Quartino Bottega Organica would be an ideal date spot—in or out of the garden.

RAW SOUL

Raw Vegan Café, Juice Bar
348 W. 145th St. (St. Nicholas &
Edgecombe St.) ① ③ Ⓐ Ⓒ Ⓑ Ⓓ
212 491-5859
rawsoul.com
Tue–Sat 11–9, Sun 12–5, closed Mon

This tiny, bare-bones raw foods eatery must have seemed an odd addition to this strip of Harlem—populated as it is with banks, Starbucks, fruit stands and sunglass hawkers—when it arrived. Though the décor is a bit wanting—green leather-topped stools are uncomfortable, and don't induce a desire to linger by any of the handful of tables—the eats are just fine, including uncommonly good sweets and shakes.

Of the starters, choose the fresh sauerkraut; Jared practically downed an entire portion of a piquant, mustard-spiked number (fermented goods are healthy, people!) solo. Though marinated greens were rather "eh," and a too-garlicky and all-collard green wrap with a bit of sundried tomato-nutmeat paste proved dull, the burgers were among the best veggie burgers—and uncooked ones!—I've eaten, sweetened up with sundried tomatoes, red onions, and a slightly addictive housemade "barbecue" sauce. Pizza, unfortunately, could have been better. Though the toppings were very fresh, the flax crust was difficult to cut through.

Wise diners will swing by at lunch for that burger—part of a $10 lunch special that includes soup and a tea—and pair it with a Yes Love Protein Shake. The oddly named potion is packed with nut milk, banana, agave, coconut butter, papaya, pineapple and hemp protein powder. With a hint of cinnamon and that swirl of tropical fruits, it's addictive. Or listen to the ladies one table over from us and snag a piece of the cheesecake. That cashew filling we've seen everywhere is impressively creamy here, and came with a stripe of ruby cranberry and curls of orange zest on top. Though it wasn't the best of the naturally sweetened desserts we tried, if the behavior of our neighbors is any indication—they demanded photos with the chef—it's worth squealing over.

This split-level restaurant feels like the love child of a celebrity spa and a modern art museum, which we suppose shouldn't shock us on the Upper East Side. Sexy two-tone white leather-and-wooden chairs nestle next to pale oak booths and wooden tables, and a plethora of bright-red tchotchkes—light boxes, a pool of cranberries,

ROUGE TOMATE
Contemporary American
10 E. 60th St.
(5th & Madison Ave.)
4 5 6 R W F
646-237-8977
rougetomatenyc.com
Daily 12–10

square candles—had us wondering whether Martha Stewart herself had just stormed through in a Valentine's Day-induced frenzy, leaving a scarlet trail in her wake. No matter. The food here is very good and quite healthy: Chef Jeremy Bearman (a Daniel Boulud alum) created a menu approved by an on-staff nutritionist. They hope to marry "well-executed cuisine" to "authentic nutrition." Okay by us!

The first collaboration we tasted, that ho hum standby squash soup, was a knockout here, lent a round, beautifully *umami* flavor by an ethereal cloud of licorice foam, with diced apples and pecans delivering a precise textural counterpoint to the silky broth. The second sampling, a fluke tartar stacked with pea shoots, squash, wakame seaweed, and pear slices, was quite good, but rather texturally overwhelming. Entrées were on more solid turf, like a skewer of toothsome venison served with garlicky mint raita and a flurry of pale golden bulgur wheat. Only a chicken entrée took another "kitchen sink" approach to texture, with extremely crunchy chestnuts, soft raisins, tart cherries and fluffy quinoa comprising an oddly chaotic bed for the bird. But that bird was shellacked golden, organic and utterly juicy, so we will admit to splitting hairs. Overall, we were happy, especially given the number of organic wines, the filtered water and the abundance of vegetable options. The icing on the cake? The seductively smooth tables and floors were stamped as eco-friendly by the Forest Stewardship Council—a small triumph of substance over style.

SACRED CHOW
Vegan Kosher Café
227 Sullivan St.
(Bleecker & W. 3rd St.)
1 A C E B D F V PATH
212 337-0863
sacredchow.com
Sun–Th 11–10, Fri–Sat 11–11

Northwest-born New Yorkers will saunter through the door of this little café and do a double-take: It's a dead ringer for any Portland, Oregon café. And brunch on our visit was—an avowed carnivore winces to type these words of a vegan eatery—fantastic.

The hippie vibe is on the premises in a major way:

Gargantuan faux-Japanese lanterns dangle overhead; the logo is of a mellow-looking cartoon cow practicing yoga; our waiter was über-friendly despite being the only one working his shift. Cynical Gothamites will have to bite their tongues at the sincerity of it all. But the delicious, 95% organic food will get them talking again. Curried tofu scramble—so egglike we experienced momentary disorientation—was served with a side of addictively smoky new potatoes that count among the best we've eaten at brunch. Spying a waffle made with spelt and oats, we ordered it and braced ourselves (spelt, though healthy, is tricky to make tasty) only to be wowed by its plushness. If I'd still been on the fence, a tiny pitcher of sweet, fresh blueberry sauce swimming with berries would have won me over. Even a side of curry-flecked steamed broccoli, and a savory tempeh reuben topped with perfectly golden, sweet caramelized onions impressed us.

Those with dietary restrictions will be pleased to see that every dish is labeled gluten-, wheat-, or sugar-free, so they can order without interrogating the waiter. Such a thing is a concern on a date, a vibe this spot also has in spades, with cushy seats by a sunny window looking like prime romantic turf. On evening outings, those who wish to can tipple on local beers like Ommegang or kosher (the place is certified), organic wines. With such abundant options, and service so gallant—our waiter dropped a stack of plates, but walked away still smiling broadly—all can seem quite right with the world.

This square, red brick-lined West Village eatery serves up eclectic American cuisine as effortless as the Marvin Gaye soundtrack swirling around its diners. From the sustainable, biodynamic and organic wines dotting the menu (I loved a bright Spanish Albariño) to a comforting rack of lamb, everything we sampled here hit the

SALT
Seasonal American
58 Macdougal St. (Prince & Houston St.) ① Ⓐ Ⓒ Ⓔ Ⓑ Ⓓ Ⓕ Ⓥ
212 674-4968
saltnyc.com
M–Th 12–3/6–11, Fri 12–3/6–12, Sat 12–4/6–12, Sun 12–4/6–10

mark. Decide when reserving a table how sociable you feel: A handful of two-tops line the windows, but long, wooden communal tables dominate the bulk of the space.

Once they settle in, carnivores will celebrate the availability of antibiotic-free meats from duck to lamb to poultry, and locavore-friendly fish will satisfy pescatarians. Vegetarian options were largely limited to the starters and sides, but they're substantial and well-executed—including crisp-on-the-outside, tender-on-the-inside roasted Brussels sprouts. Sweet stewed cherries and a tangle of caramelized onions were an ideal foil for über-healthy chicken liver mousse: It's so creamy one might think butter had been swirled into it, and features a sparkle of sea salt across the top, like waves cresting on a small pond. Whole wheat fettuccini gets the royal treatment, too, decked out with swirls of ricotta and housemade Italian sausage. As per entrées, sodium intake-watchers might ask the chef to err on the undersalting end. Lamb shank served in a dreamily savory broth was propped up on homemade merguez and plush white beans, its flesh falling pliantly off the bone, but was a shade oversalted. Bluefish pulled straight from the Long Island Sound likewise did well by us, crackly-topped and moist, and plopped on our plates atop lightly caramelized leeks. Finish the meal, if you wish, with a jolt of silky espresso from Brooklyn own's Kitten Coffee, and tip well—the waitstaff here are charmingly salt-of-the-earth types.

Melissa O'Donnell of Salt

When she opened Salt, Melissa O'Donnell had one goal: re-create the dinners of her childhood, a down-home setting where fresh and simple food was the central focus of a two-hour meal.

Fittingly, O'Donnell came up with the homey restaurant's everyday name. One, salt is a symbol of friendship in a number of cultures, where new neighbors are greeted with the essential nutrient. Two, it's the only ingredient needed to enhance the flavor when you are using high-quality ingredients.

Everything else — the sustainable meats, seasonal foods and biodynamic, organic and sustainable wines — has evolved over time.

As a classically trained cook, O'Donnell respects chefs who manipulate food using scientific techniques. But it's not her style.

"As the restaurant developed, it didn't make sense to make the food more complicated," she says. "I feel Long Island duck breast is so good. Why would I want to change it? The cauliflower soup is pretty much cauliflower. Food is so beautiful. It's so natural. I feel like the less I do, the better."

Instead, O'Donnell has focused on ingredients: sourcing sustainable fish, grass-fed beef and humanely raised pork, along with organic fruits and vegetables when they are available.

O'Donnell and her small staff create as much as possible in house, from curing bacon to stuffing casings for sausages to rolling pasta. She occasionally makes her own cheeses (mozzarella, ricotta) and breads (foccacia), and in the fall, she pickles haricot verts and onions.

If only her tiny SoHo space would allow, O'Donnell would have a garden out back and a stable to raise her own animals.

–Pervaiz Shallwani

In a true echo of its name, this restaurant feels like a haven from the hustle and bustle of nearby Canal Street. As one online reviewer boasts of the elegant, sexy space, "This is my new go-to place to take a date...the servers are so friendly it makes women feel comfortable." Indeed, the eatery was packed with the fairer sex one Sunday night, but perhaps it's the siren call of tea leaves they hear: Sanctuary Tea's menu is infused with it across the board. Even the olive oil served alongside fluffy bread is flecked with the stuff.

SANCTUARY TEA

Contemporary American
337B W. Broadway @ Grand St.
1 6 A C E J M Z N Q R W
212 941-7832
sanctuarytea.com
Sun–Th 9 am–11:30 pm,
Fri–Sat 10 am–12:30 am

So arrive in time to get a tiny two-top by the open windows, if you can, which open clean onto the street when the weather is fine. Most of the food we tried was great, particularly an organic burger slider topped with sweetly roasted tomato, slippery onion jam, and piquant baby pickles. Though the duck breast could have been a bit more tender, and a seasonal gazpacho proved uninspiring, we loved gnocchi pan-seared in brown butter served over a mélange of tender fava beans and wild mushrooms. The eclectic menu offers several vegetable sides, which pleased Jared, but we wished a few grilled veggies had received more of a slick of olive oil; they hadn't received the same care as the pillowy gnocchi. Those who drink will find plenty of wines, cocktails and beer to their liking, including Samuel Smith's organic lager and several organic vinos. Gorgeous August weather seemed to lend itself to cocktails, including a brisk champagne sangria bubbling with fresh peaches. Naturally, teas, including a few organic numbers, are abundant—dozens upon dozens of brews seem tailor-made to the seasons, whether watermelon in summer or smoky Lapsang Souchong in winter—and will no doubt have us darkening this doorway again.

SAVOY

Seasonal American
70 Prince St. @ Crosby St.
⑥ Ⓑ Ⓓ Ⓕ Ⓥ Ⓡ Ⓦ
212 219-8570
savoynyc.com
Sun 6–10, Mon–Th 12–10:30,
Fri/Sat 12–11

Peter Hoffman, chef-owner of Savoy (and owner of Back Forty, see page 83) is one of the forefathers of locally procured food. He's run his SoHo eatery this way since 1995, and puts his money where his sustainability focused mouth is: He even sources honey from hives based on the rooftops of New York City homes (hopefully not including yours). And with its proximity to a buzzing, shopping-obsessed section of downtown, this is a calming bistro in which to take refuge. Plush banquettes on the second level lend themselves to a convivial feeling, whereas downstairs feels more appropriate for a quiet business lunch, with flattering light emanating from tiny jewel-like lights suspended from silver threads.

Hoffman's menu shines with organic, antibiotic-free fare that is quite good and sometimes great. Starters, for example, knocked our socks off: A twist on ho-hum heirloom tomato salad featured not only the green, yellow and red familiars, but also ripe-as-can-be peaches, which came to fruition—forgive us—under a sparkle of icy fennel granita. It was the sort of starter that literally leaves one smiling. Equally impressive were tender morsels of lobster and sweet rings of Montauk (Long Island) squid luxuriating in a bath of mint-sweetened cucumber consommé. Our ear-to-ear grins only subsided when entrées arrived (and vegetarians, be forewarned that this menu tilts carnivorously!). Lamb was rather chewy, on a bed of sour mashed potatoes, and wild salmon arrived cold at center. Once it was cooked a touch more by an accommodating chef, we were able to fully appreciate the heart-healthy legumes that accompanied it—a delicate summer minestrone of soft elephant and pinto beans. With the caliber of fish dishes overall, pescatarians may well have found a swell night out in SoHo.

At some eateries, elegant ambiance comes easily: Gilt (page 112) is effortlessly baroque; Il Buco (page 120) oozes rustic romance. The most recent addition to David Bouley's Tribeca empire doesn't quite hit these high notes, but it's not for lack of trying. This new David Bouley space features high

SECESSION
Eclectic
30 Hudson St. (Duane & Reade St.)
① ② ③ Ⓐ Ⓒ Ⓔ Ⓡ Ⓦ
212 791-3771
davidbouley.com
Mon–Sat 5–11:30

ceilings, posh Klimt paintings and glimmering wall sconces amid oddly suburban aspects like dull mauve walls and an über-utilitarian bathroom. But give the place a chance. For one, the water is filtered. Two, meats are hormone and antibiotic-free and include several local options. Three, in any given season between 70% and 90% of the produce is local and organic. Not bad for a French eatery, especially one turning out such good food.

The epic menu is best suited to decisive diners, listing salads, terrines, meat, seafood, pasta, soups, risottos and more. Hardly knowing where to begin, we started with thick slices of duck terrine dotted with pieces of orange. It proved a little chunky, so next time we'll opt for a side of roast Brussels sprouts sprinkled with pistachios or an excellent salad in which dark cured olives perch alongside rounds of Japanese cucumber, feta, and cherry tomatoes in a piquant tarragon-infused dressing of raspberry and vanilla. Entrées were likewise head-turning, particularly thick slices of filet mignon and mashed potatoes so dreamily addictive we nearly grabbed our waiter's arm to interrogate him about them: Under pressure, he revealed that Bouley himself commissioned a strain of purple Peruvian potato based on three types he loves, and simply whips in a goodly amount of butter. Basic, sure— but brilliant. A plate of cod arrived flaky and rich, in a gingery orange sauce, sitting pretty next to a stack of thinly julienned veggies. Though its decor may not fully float our boat, when the meat and potatoes of a restaurant are this good, we'll be back.

SLICE

Pizzeria, Café
1413 2nd Ave. (73rd & 74th St.) **6**
212 249-4353
sliceperfect.com
Mon–Wed 11–10, Th–Sun 11–11

$ $ $

"Cute" being a byword in the Upper East Side, it should come as no surprise that the land of small dogs and tiny-but-pricey handbags now features a cute pizzeria. Since its produce is mostly organic and both meat and cheese are antibiotic-free, Slice is where we'll grab a quick bite after our next shopping or sightseeing outing.

Fittingly for the UES, tiny stylish touches are abundant. Bare red brick lines one wall and tiny silver-capped filament bulbs drop down unobtrusively overhead, illuminating a spare wooden bench dotted with square black leather pads. The minimalist effect is spa-meets-slice-joint. Stake your claim—seating is sparse—and saunter up to chat with a cheery staffer. The menu is unusual, dotted with barbecued chicken slices and chicken tikka masala numbers alongside basic offerings. Happily enough, those with dietary restrictions can breathe a sigh of relief, as gluten- and wheat-free options include pies with spelt and rice crusts. An honest assessment of the spelt crust finds it still a bit lacking and slightly overcooked. Honey whole wheat was better, especially in the "master sausage" slice, on which coins of cilantro-flecked all-natural chicken sausage join properly salty mozzarella and a thin, sweet marinara sauce. Of the three salads on offer, we discovered a strikingly good one. A generous bowl of organic mesclun tossed with matchstick carrots, thinly sliced cucumbers and plum tomatoes came with perhaps the best carrot-ginger dressing we discovered (and we tried lots!), huge with the punch of ginger. Toppings run the gamut here, and on our visit, broccoli, arugula, and peppers all did the trick (though we wish they'd trade in the garlic-in-a-jar for fresh; c'mon, guys!). Once the kinks of the oven are worked out, we'll cross our fingers for even nicer Slices.

Stepping into Souen is like discovering a tiny slice of California on a strip of 13th street teeming with NYU co-eds. The first thing to notice is a veritable wall of plants: Leafy greens line the woodsy, open-air terrace as well as the bustling second floor. Souen is a popular spot for work meetings as well as for students, and it's fairly mellow. It is also one of the standbys Jared recommends to clients, since everything is organic, dark greens

SOUEN
Asian Macrobiotic
28 E. 13th St. (University & 5th Ave.)
① ② ③ ④ ⑤ ⑥ L N Q R W PATH
212 627-7150
Mon–Sat 10–11, Sun 10–10

210 Sixth Ave. (Prince St.)
① A C E B D F V
212 807-7421
Mon–Sat 11:30–10:30, Sun 11:30–10
souen.net

are plentiful and desserts are naturally sweetened. Even diners who flip when they see the word "macrobiotic" on the menu will remain calm here: Seafood and sushi options are abundant, so there truly is something for everyone.

The absence of refined sugar—and even salts—becomes a comfort when digging into the uniformly clean-tasting food. Though a few dishes seemed a little lacking at first, such as the boiled-and-steamed veggies that accompanied our entrées, my palate largely adjusted to the under-salting over the course of the meal. Sure, I would have loved to douse a few things with salt, such as a pile of unappealing yams, but a creamy carrot dressing nicely balanced steamed kale, and my tuna steak speckled with white-and-black sesame seeds came with sweet, caramelized edges. Wild salmon was even better, encrusted in an otherworldly bright-red beet coating. Even our sole sushi roll was a pleasant surprise: Beautifully crisp softshell crab arrived bundled in nori with purple seaweed, avocado, cucumbers and asparagus. When Jared calls this high-energy food, I can't disagree. I was full—surprisingly so—for the rest of the day, despite having eaten very little.

SPRING STREET NATURAL

American
62 Spring St. @ Lafayette St.
6 B D F V R W
212 966-0290
springstreetnatural.com
Mon–Th 9 am–11:30 pm,
Fri 9 am–12:30 am,
Sat/Sun 10:30 am–12:30 am

Spring Street Natural is in the heart of SoHo, and feels like it: Men in skinny jeans waltz through the doors and keep their sunglasses on for the duration of brunch; hungover couples slump awaiting electrolyte delivery at bright window tables; bubbly families happily ignore them both. The eatery is designed for function, though it's pretty enough during the day, with soaring windows on

all sides letting the sun shine in. Otherwise, it has a somewhat chaotic suburban feel: Green leather-covered chairs park at wooden tables placed close together, with only a few booths for the lucky.

That said, we still like it for a midday fix of American cuisine with several vegan and vegetarian options. We swung by for brunch, when it's perhaps the most packed; sidewalk tables are stuffed with customers spying on their fellow SoHo shoppers when the weather is mild. Grub is typically solid, such as a side of garlicky sautéed spinach spritzed with lemon, and the many organic meats include a few toothsome chicken sausages (paired with maple syrup for a guilty fix). We do wish the owners would attend to a few more health-oriented details—filtered water, organic milk, non-refined sugar—so feel free to give feedback (a chef told us "customers haven't demanded organic milk yet"—hint, hint!) But tasty good-for-you foods can be found here, including organic eggs and a tower of tempeh for the snack-craving vegan—three fried sticks of protein balancing in a pool of spicy tomato and green cilantro sauces. A grass-fed New York strip steak sandwich was also pretty good, plated on toasted ciabatta with a tangle of mixed greens and a smear of lime-chile mayonnaise. Restaurants pay attention to feedback, so feel free to chat with your waiter, and perhaps help Spring Street Natural get even more Natural.

Tabla must have caused quite a stir when it landed in Madison Square in 1998. A giant, glittering oculus looms in the middle of the split-level space, causing visitors to gawk like tourists. Western-spangled "New Indian" cuisine must have seemed no less out of place to the local business crowd.

TABLA
Contemporary Indian
11 Madison Ave. @ 25th St. 6 F R W
212 889-0667
tablany.com
Main: Mon–Wed 12–2/5–9,
Th/Fri 12–2/5:30–10:30,
Sat 5:30–10:30, Sun 5–9
Bread Bar: Mon–Th 12–11,
Fri/Sat 12–11:30, Sun 5–10

Of course, Asian fusion is *de rigeur* now, and this jewel in Danny Meyer's (Shake Shack; Eleven Madison Park; The Modern) crown has since become a popular lunch spot. So for those craving cardamom, tamarind and chutney with a side of grass-fed steak or some twice-filtered water—rather unusual among its Indian eatery brethren—this is the place to be. Reserve a seat upstairs (Tabla proper) for a more formal meal—the carved emerald-and-pink ceiling is gorgeous—or, for better people watching, at the trendy and slightly bubbly Bread Bar downstairs.

$$ $

Tabla seems less adventurously piquant than on a visit several years ago, so don't be afraid to request dishes served spicy. Of starters, we liked a *chaat*, a twist on Indian street food: a flurry of grilled corn joined roasted jalapeños, mint and watercress for a sweet palate primer. Sourdough naan—healthier than the regular stuff—arrived on the table hot, impressively fluffy, and lightly coated with ghee, and a side of bright coins of yellow and green squash were creatively seasoned with the fruits coconut and kokum. Oddly, although all meat is organic, vegetarians may be even happier than carnivores here: Chicken korma meatballs sat in an aromatic stew that was underseasoned, and an entrée of fish cake wrapped in a banana leaf was bizarrely sour. But we quite enjoyed a flavor-packed steak sandwich served with bright tomato chutney.

All in all, the Bread Bar could make a fine first lunch date for busy, business-y types; the service is stellar and the fare, warming—even if your date proves chilly.

TEANY

Vegetarian, Café
90 Rivington St. (Orchard & Ludlow)
Ⓑ Ⓓ Ⓕ Ⓥ Ⓙ Ⓜ Ⓩ
212 475-9190
teany.com
Sun–Th 10–11, Fri/Sat 10 am–1 am

Moby opened this pet café with partner Kelly Tisdale in the Lower East Side in 2001, delighting locals and hipsters who wandered in to partake of the tea-centric vegetarian menu. Teany is a miniaturized space: One pretty white brick wall features cutout rectangular boxes to hold mini vases and their mini carnations, and customers park themselves at tiny silver discs of tables. It makes for good mingling, but not an ideal date, since neighbors may easily eavesdrop on a conversation.

As for the fare, we were impressed by the tea list itself, with 98 offerings from a boxy, metal-encased menu that include oolong, white, black, and both Chinese and Japanese green teas. A pot of Japanese green proved an aromatic upscale twist on the standard Chinese restaurant cuppa. Of the eats, definitely snag a salad—Teany's is among the best deals on the LES, with a flurry of crisply fresh greens, chickpeas, rounds of tomatoes, good-for-you sprouts, and unusual, crisply white cutouts of hearts of palm. Order it with the addictively savory seven-herb dressing, so creamy it is like gravy for greens. On our visit, crustless triangular tea sandwiches—one of tempeh, lettuce and tomatoes, and one of plucky pickle chutney and musty cheddar cheese—featured slightly gummy wheat bread, which left us disappointed. But this is a menu with a few hidden treasures, and all-vegan, often gluten-free baked goods, including scones, cupcakes and cakes. With its often flawless indie-rock soundtrack (Shins, Vampire Weekend, anyone?) and people watching, this is worth a stop-by for a glass of organic wine, a salad, a pot of tea or a cup of joe. Teany's self-serve coffee setup features both agave and organic milk, rare for the neighborhood. So grab a vessel of…something, and spy on the characters of the LES to your heart's content.

Sparklingly fresh produce and organic meat are the focus of this relaxed-but-refined UWS eatery, which ably takes up the mantle of locavore-centric downtown forefathers Savoy and Blue Hill. Since the elegant fare here is a little pricey, it's worth choosing your ambiance when making a reservation: On the right, behind a U-shaped, elegant bar, are clusters of cozy banquettes —rather more intimate and suitable to a date. To the left is a more formal dining room, with brighter lighting that emphasizes the light, mint-green walls and Edward Hopper-esque contemporary art.

TELEPAN

Contemporary American
72 W. 69th St. (Columbus Ave. &
Central Park West) ① ② ③ Ⓑ Ⓒ
212 580-4300
telepan-ny.com
Dinner: Mon-Th 5-11, Fri/Sat 5-11:30,
Sun 5-10:30
Lunch: Wed-Fri 11:30-2:30
Brunch: Sat/Sun 11-2:30

On both sides, Euro-flecked fare shines Chef-owner Bill Telepan has worked with such Gallic luminaries as Daniel Boulud at Le Cirque and Gilbert Le Coze at Le Bernadin, and it shows, both in a classic cheese *gougères amuse-bouche* paired with bright, flavorful gazpacho and the hearty, earthy hangar steak glazed in decadent oxtail bone-marrow sauce that ended our meal. Telepan takes the root of his food seriously, sourcing within 250 miles whenever possible.

If it's chilly outside, start with a heart warming soup. Drifts of bread float amidst pigeon peas, root vegetables and carrots in a simple, parmesan-infused vegetable broth. Move on to an unmissable lobster Bolognese—the lightest twist on that Italian classic imaginable, with chunks of the buttery crustacean swimming in a sweet tomato sauce dotted with fronds of dill. Ironically, we also ordered an entrée of "the poor man's lobster"—monkfish—in a luxurious dill-buttermilk sauce. Though it can't go tail to tail with that lobster, it was just fine—although carnivores will happily ignore all fish items and take up their sharp knives for the aforementioned steak, perhaps the most tender, well-marbled grass-fed beef we encountered. Skip dessert, if you're avoiding sugar: None are naturally sweetened (yet), though with the chef's eggs-to-apples approach to food, we'd be unsurprised to see that around the corner.

Bill Telepan of Telepan

For more than 15 years, Bill Telepan has been honing his menu to create a style he has dubbed "behind-the-scenes cooking."

On the plate, the food looks simple enough; succulent meat, a simple use of vegetables, not a lot of spices. In the kitchen it's a different matter. There are hours of preparation to create a dish that looks incredibly simple, but leaves the customer feeling as if they couldn't do it if they tried.

"I want people to think that we didn't do anything to it, but at the same time to be like 'Those are Brussels sprouts that I could never cook,'" Telepan says.

In the Telepan kitchen, it all begins on the farm where he has been developing close relationships with the farmers who raise his food.

He likes to call his sourcing of ingredients hyper-seasonal, which entails grasping the times of year when a particular ingredient is at its best, (such as gooseberries, which are only in season for three weeks) and showcasing them on the menu in that time span.

Telepan and his chefs have developed a knack for bringing out the best in each ingredient using techniques and seasoning — searing, braising, the right amount of salt, oil, butter.

It helps that Telepan has an educated clientele that have developed a thirst for his changing menu. "It's basically become mainstream, especially with people who have become interested in food. They demand it. They look forward to it."   –Pervaiz Shallwani

A number of West Village restaurants clamor for the title of "romantic date place." This eatery tries really, really hard, with superlatively rustic touches that include wide, flat stones on the walls, a fake fireplace, and two terraces illuminated by tiny lights. For the most part, the schtick works. And when the fare is all-organic

THE PLACE
American
310 W. 4th St. (Bank & 12th St.)
① ② ③ Ⓛ Ⓐ Ⓒ Ⓔ Ⓕ Ⓥ PATH
212 924-2711
theplaceny.com
M–Fri 11:30–3.30/5:30–11,
Sat/Sun 10:30–4/5:30–11

right down to the fluffy bread served before dinner—and it's this good—we have few complaints (though we admit we wish filtered water and organic wines were on offer).

The food is "new American," with nods to France (hello, butter sauces!) and Italy (made-on the-premises pasta). Start with duck pappardelle; though the slim, wide noodles were a little wobbly for our taste, shreds of organic duck confit— served ragout-style in a sweet tomato sauce with artichoke hearts under a powder of parmigiano reggiano—made this more successful than its pasta counterpart of four teeny squash ravioli overwhelmed by a brown butter sauce. Entrées are what shine here, and happily, they're plated with oodles of vegetables. A bright clash of grilled wild salmon sits smugly on a bed of tender-but-crunchy spears of asparagus and jewel-hued beets. Butter makes an encore in the white wine-spiked sauce pooling under the succulent, fork-tender fish. Leg of lamb was nearly as good, and would especially please those who find lamb a bit "gamy"—the *jus* adds a dark, rich, almost soylike flavor, and gives a savory charge to both tender slices of the beast and a mélange of sautéed summer squash and spinach. Aside from the veggie-packed plates, Jared was pleased by the presence of flat parsley in several dishes, as it's packed with iron and vitamins. Since this chef doesn't overwhelm his plates with it, seeming to know the herb's proper, er, Place, a foodie would hold her protests.

24 CARROTS

Juice Bar, Vegetarian Deli
244 W. 72nd St.
(Broadway & West End Ave.)
212 595-2550
24carrotsnyc.com
Daily 9–10

Don't be alarmed by its chirpily healthy name, and resist the urge to declare, "I will *not* be eating twenty-four carrots for lunch, thank you very much," because—believe it or not—this tiny "to-go" joint is essentially a Babycakes (page 82) outpost on the Upper West Side.

Visitors peering through the window of the deli-slash-juice bar will spy a wall lined with vitamins, bins of bananas and apples in the front, and a daunting smoothie sign bearing a giant carrot. It'd be easy for them to overlook tasty sweets culled from a few of the city's best natural sweetener-focused bakeries, including Raw Soul's chocolate cheesecake (see page 140) and beloved downtown sweets shack Babycakes' addictive banana chocolate-chip bread (see page 82). Over half a dozen of the Baby's goods were on offer: Gluten-free gingersnaps were spicy and snappy as can be, and Florida crystal-sweetened double-chocolate cookies vanished down our gullets in a flash. We even spotted the Babycake cupcakes, with that signature pastel flower curled invitingly on top. (Those who demand fresh cupcakes should swing by when deliveries arrive on Tuesday, Thursday and Saturday.) The sugarless high doesn't end there, however: In the freezer lurk local Organic Nectars gelatos. Mint chip, though not as amazing as Pure Food and Wine's, was sweet, sexily smooth and darn impressive for an agave-sweetened dairy-free ice cream.

Savories were a bit more hit-or-miss. Artichoke-noodle lasagna was fine, layered with a savory tomato sauce and thinly sliced zucchini and squash, but soups were largely a disappointment, as was tart spinach-and-spelt phyllo pie. But juices were lovely, including a subtle gingery apple-pear-lemon elixir, so snag one, and get everything to go: There are only two seats in the place (all the better to scarf down these not-so-forbidden sweets at home—or, if you can't wait, on the street).

This slim, bright-orange eatery has been serving organic, mostly vegan fare to midtown worker bees and denizens since 2000 (before it was trendy!) Owner Mark Mager is a charismatic force behind the counter, doling out handshakes to regulars and peppering his menu with exclamations like, "I promise you'll love it!"

UNCLE MARKY'S ORGANICS
Café, Juice Bar
235 E. 53rd St. (2nd & 3rd Ave.)
④ ⑤ ⑥ Ⓔ Ⓥ Ⓝ Ⓡ Ⓦ
212 421-6444
unclemarkysorganics.com
M–Fri 11–9:30, Sat/Sun 12–9

By and large, we do: Sparklingly fresh soups, salads, wraps and entrées are all offered and, although we'd never take a date here (only a handful of stools line the tiny spot), it's ideal for takeout, delivery or a quick bite at the counter. Mager's interest in healthy eating—he's a graduate of the National Gourmet Institute for Culinary Health—shines in a kaleidoscopic menu, featuring vegan, macrobiotic and raw options, with all-natural options for meat eaters like wild salmon, grass-fed beef and free-range chicken. Cooks only use premium, heart-friendly cooking oils, such as coconut and olive, and all of the homemade desserts are vegan and sweetened with agave nectar. We only give "Marky" a rap on the knuckles when it comes to bread: He uses standard multigrain buns instead of those made from sprouted grain.

The chef here has a fairly broad repertoire, succeeding with a kicky gazpacho, three succulent beef tacos drizzled with pico de gallo, and an autumnal "triple protein bonanza," a lasagna-like layered creation of tempeh, tofu and quinoa drizzled with a sweet curry sauce. Jared's favorite dish here is a pleasantly flaky slab of wild salmon served simply with brown rice and sautéed kale. Monastic, but it works. Treats—most of which are vegan, wheat-free, and agave-sweetened—are a bit more hit-or-miss: Tofu cheesecake tasted like it sounds, but chocolate cake crusted with coconut curls was surprisingly good. Overall, it seems Uncle Marky has something to be excited about.

VIVA HERBAL PIZZERIA

Vegetarian Kosher Pizzeria
179 2nd Ave. (11th & 12th St.)
6 L R W
212 420-8801
Daily 11–11:30

$

This vegetarian pizza joint has been turning out pies to East Village denizens and bar-crawlers for a little over a decade now. Most produce is organic and cheese is both kosher and hormone-free, making this a more salubrious slice option than its neighboring competitors. Decor is slightly lacking, with a few chairs strewn about, a couple of unsteady red metal tables, and a spooky, lockless bathroom in the back of the restaurant. So snag your slice "to go" if you're looking for ambiance.

The pizza is solid, with an extraordinary variety of crusts on offer that include unbleached white, whole wheat, cornmeal and even spelt. The latter, for those unaccustomed to it, is a red grain that provides a certain earthiness to dough. It's much better for you than whole wheat or white, and at Viva it adds a density of flavor to a simple trio of mozzarella, spinach and tomato toppings. Fans of nearby Two Boots should sample the cornmeal crust, but should avoid the "Mexicali" number unless they can really stand the heat: A bevy of toppings include chopped cilantro, onions, tomatoes and an onslaught of take-no-prisoners jalapeños. I preferred a simple margarita slice—very good on traditional dough, and totally fine on whole wheat—but pizza-topping options are kaleidoscopic, including broccoli, roast peppers and "green tea herbed miso-tofu," so load up on veggie toppings.

Note that this is Gotham we're talking about, and these slices may not win awards among purists. But with vegan options, pesticide-free produce and healthier drinks like naturally sweetened sodas to provide a welcome respite from the typical Coke-slinging pizzeria, this is a wise move for hungry wanderers in a pinch. Call ahead and snag a pie made to order and lug it home or to nearby Thompson Square Park. It'd be very New York of you.

This Village restaurant can be summed up in two words: Celebrity Central. *US Weekly* readers will love it for the people watching, and since the meats are organic and the fare is fine, we approve.

THE WAVERLY INN
Seasonal American
16 Bank St. @ Waverly Pl.
① ② ③ Ⓛ Ⓐ Ⓒ Ⓔ Ⓕ Ⓥ PATH
212 243-7900 (always busy)
Sun–Mon 6–11:45 , Tue–Sat 6–12:45

No phone number is listed, so swing by in your most casual designer duds and ignore the fact that restaurant owner (and *Vanity Fair* editor) Graydon Carter has made reservations nearly as difficult as entrée to his famous Oscar parties. We managed to snag an early reservation, and sauntered through the rustic front room as slowly as possible to gawk at Mario Batali and family (is he following us? see page 84) before being hustled to the back garden unfondly called "Siberia" by food writers. To soften the blow, I sipped a glass of delicious cherry-laden biodynamic Pinot Noir from Robert Sinskey while eyeballing a menu stuffed with American comfort food. Though this is strange for a place with such a floor show, the chef largely succeeds. A serviceable Waldorf salad is dotted with purple grapes and cubes of apple. Though an appetizer size portion of earthy shortribs didn't quite wow us—it was slightly mismatched with its topping of diced celery, carrot and onion—service and entrées compensated. Our sweetheart of a waiter had suggested the chicken pot pie, which "Martha had on her show—if she likes it, you know it's good!" It was, though not earth-shattering. Puff pastry crust bears a glossy sheen and a dusting of salt and pepper, but the filling was dense with cream, chicken and not many veggies. Better was the wild king salmon with a nice peachy hue, a slew of beluga lentils—black and gleaming, like their namesake—and a tumble of Tuscan kale. Speaking of sparkle, make the most of your exit: It's your last chance to see the Who's Who inside this eatery before being politely escorted out.

WHOLE FOODS
Eclectic
Multiple Locations
wholefoodsmarket.com

Ah, Whole Foods. Is it a store? A meeting place? A shrine? Whatever it is, the grocery behemoth renowned for its all-natural foods has its fans, and they contribute to the five Gotham locations feeling like madhouses much of the time.

It's a boon, then, that each Whole Foods has its own "restaurant," so you can squirrel your finds—whether organic greens, gluten-free cookies or a tasty antibiotic-free chicken soup—back to a table. The Columbus Circle location boasts a cacophonous but fun caféteria and juice bar; the Bowery shop sports a calmer second-level eatery with electrical outlets accessible to laptop-luggers. We swung by the Bowery location, where I love to lurk in the adjacent Beer Room to snag tap suds like upstate's Captain Lawrence Liquid Gold poured into recyclable growlers "to go." If swinging by for a quick bite, the Bowery's faux-"trattoria" offers perfectly serviceable pasta that includes a few wheat noodle numbers and pumpkin ravioli in brown butter sauce flecked with sage. The salad bar almost always boasts a few treasures—at the Columbus Circle spot, organic chicken tikka masala has been the bomb on several occasions—and at the Bowery store, the salad bar was packed with good stuff—lentils here, a super-fresh mixed-green salad there. As per desserts, wheat- and gluten-free options are available in the bakery. Just be sure—no matter which salad, sushi or dessert bar you're at—you read the ingredients listed over each offering. Watch out for sugar! Not so healthy, people. Although if you're going for cheese, this is the place to shop for it: Tons of organic *fromage* is on offer, and most is hormone-free. No wonder people love this place. And truly, it's satisfying to break with social mores and eat at the grocery store: At Whole Foods, it's safe to shop hungry.

270 Greenwich St. @ Murray St.

①②③Ⓐ ⒸⒺ PATH

(212) 349-6555

Daily 8am-10pm

95 E Houston St. @ Bowery

⑥ⒷⒹⒻⓋ

(212) 420-1320

Daily 8am-11pm

10 Columbus Circle

Suite SC101

(Broadway & Central Park West)

(212) 823-9600

Daily 8am-11pm

4 Union Square East @ 14th St.

④⑤⑥ⓁⓃⓆⓇⓌ

212 673-5388

Daily 8am-11pm

250 7th Ave.

①ⒻⓋ PATH

(24th & 25th St.)

(212) 924-5969

Daily 8am-11pm

ZEST

Café, Salad Bar
1441 Broadway (40th and 41st)
① ② ③ Ⓢ ⑦ Ⓝ Ⓠ Ⓡ Ⓦ
Ⓐ Ⓒ Ⓔ Ⓑ Ⓓ Ⓕ Ⓥ PATH
212 398-9378
zestnyc.com
Mon–Fri 7 am–9 pm

The Times Square area is not renowned for inducing that Zen feeling in visitors and locals, and worker bees in this neck of the woods often feel strapped when hunting healthy fare. Happily, there's Zest, a takeaway-focused salad, sandwich and hot entrée lunch joint that succeeds where a number of vegetarian-focused eateries fail. Not only is it cheap, it's cute: Large orange lanterns illuminate a row of white, clean tables behind an extensive cold appetizer bar, and—even when crowded—the eatery feels fairly chill. For the most part, the cooks seem to know what they're doing: Red cabbage cole slaw gets a snap from fresh ginger and is sensibly under-mayo'ed and under-vinegared. Pair it with some deliciously chilly soba noodles, sesame seed-speckled sautéed broccoli or an addictive pile of edamame sparkling with corn. And note we said "vegetarian-focused:" Organic beef and chicken are both on offer, and the salmon is wild. Chicken quesadilla fans will be happy to note that there's a great one on offer here, and it's stuffed with lean bits of bird, snappy green onions and cilantro, and served with a fiery, made-on-the-premises chipotle salsa. The one premade sandwich we tried—wild salmon, ginger, with that same great slaw—wasn't a perfect combo, but most options were excellent, so we suggest poking through the menu until you find what you like. Jared happily noted organic ingredients across the menu, and sorbet and yogurt smoothies packed with fruit without added sugar. Perhaps this is why we observed customers walk out looking generally perkier than when they walked in.

SUPPLEMENTAL LISTS

Great Health-Food Markets

Here's a round-up of my favorite markets—by which I mean health-food stores and juice bars—in Manhattan. Bold type indicates that the market serves prepared foods and includes seating, making it a fast, casual dining-out option.

Bell Bates
97 Reade St. (at Broadway)
212 267-4300
bellbates.com

Earthmatters
177 Ludlow (below Houston St.)
212 475-4180
earthmatters.com

Fairway
2328 12th Avenue
(132nd & 133rd St.)
212 234-3883
fairwaymarket.com

2127 Broadway (74th & 75th St.)
212 595-1888

Gary Null's
2421 Broadway (89th & 90th St.)
212 874-4000

High Vibe
138 E 3rd St. (1st Ave. & Avenue A)
212 777-6645
highvibe.com

Integral Yoga
229 W 13th St.
(7th & Greenwich Ave.)
212 243-2642
integralyoganaturalfoods.com

Lifethyme
410 6th Avenue (8th & 9th St.)
212 420-9099
lifethymemarket.com

Live Live
261 E 10th Street
(Ave. A & First Ave.)
212 505-5504
live-live.com

Organic Avenue
101 Stanton Street
(Ludlow & Orchard St.)
212 334-4593
organicavenue.com

43 Eighth Avenue
(Jane & Horatio St.)
212 675-3672

Organic Market
275 7th Avenue @ 26th St.
212 243-9927

Trader Joe's
> 142 E 14th St.
> (4th Ave. & Irving Pl.)
> 212 529-4612
> traderjoes.com

Westerly's
> 913 8th Ave. (54th & 55th St.)
> 212 586-5262
> westerlyhealthfoods.com

Whole Foods Market
> **270 Greenwich St. @ Murray St.**
> **212 349-6555**
> **wholefoodsmarket.com**

> **95 E Houston St. @ Bowery**
> **212 420-1320**

> **10 Columbus Circle**
> **Suite SC101**
> **(Broadway & W Central Park)**
> **212 823-9600**

> **4 Union Square E @ 14th St.**
> **212 673-5388**

> 250 7th Ave.
> (24th & 25th St.)
> 212 924-5969

Healthy Honorable Mentions

I visited all of the restaurants on this list; they passed my health standards but not our taste criteria (especially compared to other places in similar categories). However, I wanted to give you a few additional healthy-eating options. Who knows, maybe you'll disagree with me and think the dishes are delicious! Bold type indicates restaurants that I think are particularly worth a try.

Belcourt
> Mediterranean, New American
> ⓘ ⓘ ⓢ
> 84 E 4th St. @ 2nd Ave.
> 212 979-2034
> belcourtnyc.com

Beppe
> Italian ⓘ ⓘ ⓢ
> 45 E 22nd St.
> (Broadway & Park Ave. S)
> 212 982-8422
> beppenyc.com

Café Fresh
American Café ● ●
1241 Amsterdam Ave. @ 121st St.
212 222-6340
gofreshnyc.com

Corner Shop Café
New American, Traditional
American ● ● ●
643 Broadway @ Bleecker St.
212 253-7467
cornershopcafé.com

Employees Only
New American ● ● ●
510 Hudson St.
(10th & Christopher St.)
212 242-3021
employeesonlynyc.com

Friend of a Farmer
Traditional American ● ●
77 Irving Pl (18th & 19th St.)
212 477-2188
friendofafarmernyc.com

Great Jones Spa and Juice Bar
Cafe and Juice Bar ●
29 Great Jones St.
212 505-3185
greatjonesspa.com

Good Health
Vegetarian ● ●
1435 1st Ave. (74th & 75th St.)
212 517-9898

Good Health Burger
Vegetarian ● ●
237 E 53rd St. (2nd & 3rd Ave.)
212 888-8007

Gusto Grilled Organics
Argentinian ● ●
519 Sixth Avenue
(13th and 14th St.)
212 242-5800
gustoorganics.com

Irving Mill
New American ● ●
116 E 16th St.
(Union Square E & Irving Pl.)
212 254-1600
irvingmill.com

Jane
New American ● ● ●
100 W Houston St.
(Thompson St. & LaGuardia Pl.)
212 254-7000
janerestaurant.com

Jivamuktea Café
Vegan ● ●
841 Broadway 2nd floor
(13th & 14th St.)
212 353-0214
jivamuktiyoga.com

Jubbs Longevity
Live, Raw Food ● ●
508 E 12th St. @ Avenue A
212 353-5015
jubbslongevity.com

The Kitchen Club
 Eclectic ●●●
 30 Prince St. @ Mott St.
 212 274-0025
 thekitchenclub.com

Lever House
 New American, French ●●●●
 390 Park Ave. @ 53rd St.
 212 888-2700
 leverhouse.com

Little Lad's
 Vegetarian ●
 120 Broadway @ Cedar St.
 212 227-5744
 littlelads.net

Marc and Blue Café
 New American ●●
 973 Columbus Avenue @ 108th St.
 212 222-2033
 marcandblue.com

Organic Grill
 Vegetarian ●●
 123 1st Ave.
 (7th St. & St. Marks Pl.)
 212 477-7177
 theorganicgrill.com

Ozu
 Macrobiotic, Kosher ●●
 566 Amsterdam Ave.
 (87th & 88th St.)
 212 787-8316
 ozunyc.com

PicNic
 French ●●●
 2665 Broadway
 (101st and 102nd St.)
 212 222-8222
 picnicmarket.com

Quantum Leap
 Vegetarian ●●
 226 Thompson St.
 (Bleecker & W 3rd St.)
 212 677-8050
 quantumleaprestaurant.com

 203 1st Ave. (12th & 13th St.)
 212 673-9848

Quintessence
 Raw Vegan ●●
 263 E 10th St.
 (Avenue A & 1st Ave.)
 646-654-1823
 raw-q.com

Sal Anthony's Raw Bar
 Raw Vegan ●●
 119 E 17th St.
 (Park Ave. S & Irving Pl.)
 212 647-6677
 salanthonys.com

Sixth Street Community Center
 Vegetarian ●
 638 E Sixth Street
 (Avenue B & Avenue C)
 212 677-1863
 http://sixthstreetcenter.org

'SNice
  Vegetarian ⬤⬤
  45 8th avenue
  (Jane & W 4th St.)
  212 645-0310
Strictly Roots
  Caribbean, Vegetarian ⬤
  2058 Adam Clayton Powell Blvd.
  @ 123rd St.
  212 864-8699
  strictlyroots.net
Temple in The Village
  Vegetarian ⬤
  74 W 3rd St.
  (Laguardia Pl. & Thompson St.)
  212 475-5670
Thalassa
  Greek, Mediterranean, Seafood
  ⬤⬤⬤⬤
  179 Franklin St.
  (Greenwich & Hudson St.)
  212 941-7661
  thalassanyc.com
Tsampa
  Tibetan ⬤⬤
  212 E 9th (2nd & 3rd Ave.)
  212 614-3226

Union Square Café
  New American, Italian ⬤⬤⬤
  21 E 16th St.
  (5th Ave. & Union Square W)
  212 243-4020
  unionsquarecafé.com
Village Natural
  Vegetarian ⬤⬤
  46 Greenwich Ave. (6th & 7th Ave.)
  212 727-0968
Whole Earth Bakery
  Vegan Bakery ⬤
  130 Saint Marks Pl.
  (Avenue A and 1st Ave.)
  212 677-7597
Zaitzeff
  Burgers, Sandwiches ⬤⬤
  18 Avenue B @ 2nd St.
  212 477-7137
  zaitzeffnyc.com

  72 Nassau St. @ John St.
  212 571-7272

Tasty Honorable Mentions

Alex and I didn't eat at most of the restaurants on this list because they didn't pass the initial health screening, conducted over the phone. Most of them do offer a few sustainably-raised animal products—just not enough to make it into our featured 75. Other reasons for their exclusion may have been one or more of the following: an inadequate number of vegetable options; an overabundance of poor-quality cooking methods like frying; too many poor-quality ingredients, such as table salt and unfiltered water; and a high percentage of unhealthful foods in general, such as veal, foie gras and shellfish. Nevertheless, most of these establishments are well-known for serving delicious meals, and many are beginning to make an effort to include healthier options. Just make sure to choose carefully and cautiously from their menus.

Accademia Di Vino
Italian ●●●
1081 3rd Ave. (63rd & 64th St.)
212 888-6333
accademiadivino.com

Adour Alain Ducasse @ St. Regis Hotel
French ●●●●
2 E 55th St. New York @ 5th Ave.
212 710-2277
adour-stregis.com

Alias
New American ●●●
76 Clinton St. @ Rivington St.
212 505-5011
aliasrestaurant.com

Arabelle @ The Hotel Plaza Athenee
French ●●●●
37 E 64th St. @ Madison Ave.
212 606-4647
arabellerestaurant.com

Aroma
Italian ●●●
36 E 4th St.
(Bowery & Lafayette St.)
212 375-0100
aromanyc.com

Artisinal Fromagerie
French Bistro ●●●
2 Park Ave. @ 32nd St.
212 725-8585

Balthazaar
French Bistro ●●●
80 Spring St.
(Broadway & Crosby St.)
212 965-1414
balthazarny.com

Barbetta
Italian ⬤⬤⬤
321 W 46th St. (8th & 9th Ave.)
212 246-9171
barbettarestaurant.com

Barbounia
Greek ⬤⬤⬤
250 Park Avenue South
(19th & 20th St.)
212 995-0242
barbounia.com

Beacon
New American ⬤⬤⬤
25 W 56th St. (5th & 6th Ave.)
212 332-0500
beaconnyc.com

Bellavitae
Italian, Tapas ⬤⬤⬤
24 Minetta Ln.
(6th Ave. & MacDougal St.)
212 473 5121
bellavitae.com

Birdbath
Bakery ⬤
223 1st Ave. (13th St. & 14th St.)
646-722-6565
buildagreenbakery.com

175 7th Ave. (11th St. & S 7 Ave.)
646-722-6570

Bistro Le Steak
French, Steakhouse ⬤⬤⬤
1309 3rd Ave. (74th & 75th St.)
212 517-3800
bistrolesteak.com

Boqueria
Spanish, Tapas ⬤⬤⬤
53 W 19th St. (5th & 6th Ave.)
212 255-4160
boquerianyc.com

171 Spring St.
(Thompson St. & W Broadway)
212 343-4255

BRGR
Burgers ⬤
287 7th Ave. (26th & 27th St.)
212 488-7500
brgr.us

Brown Café
New American ⬤⬤⬤
61 Hester St. (Ludlow & Essex St.)
212 477-2427
greenbrownorange.com

Café Boulud
French, Eclectic ⬤⬤⬤
20 E 76th St. (Madison & 5th Ave.)
212 772-2600
danielnyc.com

Café Luxembourg
French Bistro 🔵🔵🔵
200 W 70th St.
(Amsterdam & West End Ave.)
212 873-7411
caféluxembourg.com

Chanterelle
French 🔵🔵🔵🔵
2 Harrison St.
(Hudson and Staple St.)
212 966-6960
chanterellenyc.com

Chiyono
Japanese 🔵🔵🔵
328 E 6th St. (1st & 2nd Ave.)
212 673-3984
chiyono.com

Ciao For Now
Café 🔵
504 E 12th St.
(Avenue A & Avenue B)
212 677-2616
ciaofornow.net

Clinton Street Baking Company
American 🔵🔵🔵
4 Clinton St.
(Stanton & Houston St.)
646-602-6263
clintonstreetbaking.com

Craft
New American 🔵🔵🔵🔵
43 E 19th St.
(Broadway & Park Ave. S)
212 780-0880
craftrestaurant.com

Craftbar
New American 🔵🔵🔵
900 Broadway @ 20th St.
212 461-4300
craftrestaurant.com

Crisp
Sandwiches, Middle Eastern 🔵
684 3rd Ave. (43rd & 44th St.)
212 661-0000
eatatcrisp.com

Daniel
French 🔵🔵🔵🔵
60 E 65th St.
(Madison & Park Ave.)
212 288-0033
danielnyc.com

Degustation
French, Spanish, Tapas 🔵🔵🔵🔵
239 E 5th St. (Bowery & 2nd Ave.)
212 979-1012

Del Posto
Italian 🔵🔵🔵🔵
85 10th Ave. (15th & 16th St.)
212 497-8090
delposto.com

East West Books Café
Vegan Café 🟢
78 5th Ave. (13th St. & 14th St.)
212 243-5994
eastwestnyc.com

Empanada Joe's
Argentinean, Fast Food 🟢
2857 Broadway @ 111th St.
212 678-0022
empanadajoes.com

683 8th Ave. (43rd & 44th St.)
212 977-2600

668 6th Ave. (21st & 22nd St.)
917-338-4780

Esca
Seafood, Italian 🟢🟢🟢🟢
402 W 43rd St. @ 9th Ave.
212 564-7272
esca-nyc.com

57 @ Four Seasons Hotel
New American 🟢🟢🟢
57 E 57th St.
(Madison & Park Ave.)
212 758-5700
fourseasons.com

5 Ninth
New American 🟢🟢
5 9th Ave.
(Gansevoort & Little West 12th St.)
212 929-9460
5ninth.com

Fleur De Sel
French 🟢🟢🟢🟢
5 E 20th St. (5th Ave. & Broadway)
212 460-9100
fleurdeselnyc.com

Four Seasons
New American 🟢🟢🟢🟢
99 E 52nd St. (Park & Lexington Ave.)
212 754-9494
fourseasonsrestaurant.com

Frog
French, Eclectic 🟢🟢🟢
71 Spring St. (Crosby & Lafayette St.)
212 966-5050
frognyc.com

Galaxy Global Eatery
New American, Eclectic 🟢🟢
15 Irving Pl. @ 15th St.
212 777-3631
galaxyglobaleatery.com

goodburger
Burgers 🟢
800 2nd Ave. @ 43rd St.
212 922-1700
goodburgerny.com

636 Lexington Ave. @ 54th St.
212 838-6000

23 W 45th St. (5th & 6th Ave.)
212 354-0900

870 Broadway (17th & 18th St.)
212 529-9100

Gordon Ramsay @ The London Hotel NYC
French ●●●●
151 W 54th St. (6th & 7th Ave.)
212 468-8888
gordonramsay.com

Hacienda de Argentina
Argentinean, Steakhouse ●●●
339 E 75th St. (1st & 2nd Ave.)
Phone: 212 472-5300
haciendadeargentina.com

Harrison
New American ●●●
355 Greenwich St. @ Harrison St.
212 274-9310
theharrison.com

'ino
Café & Winebar ●●
Italian, Sandwiches
21 Bedford St.
(6th Ave. & Downing St.)
212 989-5769
caféino.com

Inoteca
Italian, Sandwiches ●●
98 Rivington St. @ Ludlow St.
212 614-0473
inotecanyc.com

Inside Park Café @ St. Barts
New American ●●●
109 E 50th St. @ Park Ave.
212 593-3333
insideparknyc.com

Isabella's
New American ●●●
359 Columbus Ave. @ 77th St.
212 724-2100
brguestrestaurants.com

Ivo and Lulu
French, Caribbean ●●●
558 Broome St. @ Varick St.
212 226-4399

Juice Generation
Juice Bars & Smoothies ●
644 9th Ave. (45th & 46th St.)
212 541-5600
juicegeneration.com

117 W 72nd St.
(Broadway & Columbus Ave.)
212 579-0400

2730 Broadway (104th & 105th St.)
212 531-3111

171 W 4th St. (6th & 7th Ave.)
212 242-0440

Jean Georges @ Trump International Hotel and Tower
French ●●●●
1 Central Park W @ 60th St.
212 299-3900
jean-georges.com

Jewel Bako
Japanese, Sushi ●●●●
239 E 5th St. (2nd & 3rd Ave.)
212 979-1012

Kamui Den
　　Japanese, Sushi ○○
　　186 Avenue A (11th & 12th St.)
　　212 777-2096

Kate's Joint
　　Vegetarian ○○
　　58 Avenue B @ 4th St.
　　212 777-7059

Le Bernardin
　　French, Seafood ○○○○
　　155 W 51st St. (6th & 7th Ave.)
　　212 554-1515
　　le-bernardin.com

Little Giant
　　New American
　　85 Orchard St. @ Broome St.
　　212 226-5047
　　littlegiantnyc.com

Mae Mae
　　Café and Wine Bar ○○
　　86 Vandam St.
　　(Greenwich St. & Hudson St.)
　　212 924-5104

Market Table
　　New American ○○○
　　54 Carmine St. @ Bedford St.
　　212 255-2100
　　markettablenyc.com

Marumi
　　Japanese, Sushi ○○
　　546 Laguardia Pl.
　　(Bleecker & W 3rd St.)
　　212 979-7055

Molyvos
　　Greek, Seafood ○○○
　　871 7th Ave. (55th & 56th St.)
　　212 582-7500
　　molyvos.com

Momofuku Ko
　　Asian, New American ○○○○
　　163 1st Ave. @ 10th St.
　　212 475-7899
　　momofuku.com

Momofuku Noodle Bar
　　Noodle Shop, Japanese, Pan-Asian
　　○○○
　　171 1st Ave. (10th & 11th St.)
　　212 777-7773
　　momofuku.com

Momofuku Ssam Bar
　　Korean, Pan-Asian ○○○
　　207 2nd Ave. @ 13th St.
　　212 254-3500
　　momofuku.com

New York Burger Co
　　Burgers ○
　　303 Park Ave. S (23rd & 24th St.)
　　212 254-2727
　　newyorkburgerco.com

　　678 6th Ave. (21st & 22nd St.)
　　212 229-1404

Oceana

Seafood, New American

◎◎◎◎

55 E 54th St.

(Madison & Park Ave.)

212 759-5941

oceanarestaurant.com

Opus

Italian, Pizza ◎◎◎

Gluten Free Options)

1574 2nd Ave. @ 82nd St.

212 772-2220

opusrestaurantnyc.com

Otto

Italian, Pizza ◎◎

1 5th Ave. @ 8th St.

212 995-9559

ottopizzeria.com

Payard

French Bistro ◎◎◎

1032 Lexington Ave.

(73rd & 74th St.)

212 717-5252

payard.com

Per Se

French, New American ◎◎◎◎

10 Columbus Circle (Time Warner Center 4th Floor) @ 60th St.

212 823-9335

perseny.com

Persimmon

Korean ◎◎◎

277 E 10th St. (Ave. A & 1st Ave.)

212 260-9080

Picholine

French, Mediterranean ◎◎◎◎

35 W 64th St.

(Broadway & Central Park W)

212 724-8585

picholinenyc.com

Pita Joe

Middle Eastern ◎

2 W 14th @ 5th Ave.

212 627-7877

pitajoe.com

Porchetta

Sandwiches ◎◎

110 E 7th St. (1st Ave. & Avenue A)

212 777-2151

The Pump

Health Food, Sandwiches ◎

40 W 55th St. (5th & 6th Ave.)

212 246-6844

thepumpenergyfood.com

31 E 21st St.

(Park Ave. & Broadway)

212 253-7676

112 W 38th St.

(6th Ave. & Broadway)

212 764-2100

275 Madison Ave. @ 40th St.

212 697-7867

Punch

New American, Eclectic ⬤⬤
913 Broadway (20th & 21st St.)
212 673-6333
punchrestaurant.com

Red Eye Grill

American ⬤⬤⬤
890 7th Ave. (56th St. & 57th St.)
212 541-9000
redeyegrill.com

Restaurant Hearth

New American, Italian ⬤⬤⬤
403 E 12th St. @ First Ave.
646-602-1300
restauranthearth.com

Resto

Belgian ⬤⬤⬤
111 E 29th St.
(Park & Lexington Ave.)
212 685-5585
restonyc.com

Ronnybrook Farm @ the Chelsea Market

Ice Cream ⬤
75 9th Ave. @ 16th St.
212 741-6455
ronnybrookmilkbar.com

Simple Kitchen

New American ⬤⬤
361 W 17th St. (8th and 9th Ave.)
212 924-0600
simplekitchenco.com

Spotted Pig

English, New American, Eclectic ⬤⬤⬤
314 W 11th St. @ Greenwich St.
212 620-0393
thespottedpig.com

Suba

Spanish, Tapas ⬤⬤⬤
109 Ludlow St.
(Rivington & Delancey St.)
212 982-5714
subanyc.com

Suenos

Mexican ⬤⬤⬤
311 W 17th St. (8th & 9th Ave.)
212 243-1333
suenosnyc.com

Sumile Sushi

Japanese, Sushi, French ⬤⬤⬤
154 W 13th St. (6th & 7th Ave.)
212 989-7699
sumile.com

The Odeon

French, Bistro, Traditional American ⬤⬤⬤
145 W Broadway @ Thomas St.
212 233-0507
theodeonrestaurant.com

The Red Head

Traditional American, Southern & Soul ⬤⬤⬤
349 E 13th St. (1st & 2nd Ave.)
212 533-6212
theredheadnyc.com

Tocqueville

New American, French ●●●

1 E 15th St. @ 5th Ave.

212 647-1515

tocquevillerestaurant.com

Town @ The Chambers Hotel

New American ●●●

15 W 56th St. (5th & 6th Ave.)

212 582-4445

townrestaurant.com

TSalon

Sandwiches, Other ●●

11 E 20th St.

(Broadway & Park Ave. S)

212 358-0506

tsalon.com

75 Ninth Ave. @ 15th @ Chelsea market

212 243-0432

21 Club

New American ●●●

21 W 52nd St. (5th & 6th Ave.)212 582-7200

21club.com

Wallse

Austrian ●●●

344 W 11th St. @ Washington St.

212 352-2300

wallserestaurant.com

wd-50

New American, Eclectic

●●●●

50 Clinton St.

(Stanton & Rivington St.)

212 477-2900

wd-50.com

Wildwood BBQ

Barbecue ●●

225 Park Ave. S @ 18th St.

212 533-2500

brguestrestaurants.com

Yaffa Café

Vegetarian ●●

97 Saint Marks Pl.

(1st Ave. & Avenue A)

212 677-9001

yaffacafé.com

GLOSSARY

Berkshire Pork: Berkshire refers to a specific breed of pig that is known for its flavor and texture. It may or may not be raised in a sustainable fashion.

Biodynamic: Most often seen in reference to wine, it is essentially a holistic method of agriculture based on the philosophy that all aspects of the farm should be treated as an interrelated whole, never using synthetic chemicals and relying on ecologically sound farming practices often more stringent than organic requirements.

Brandt: Refers to a single-family owned beef producer that raises its animals naturally, free of antibiotics and hormones. The cows are fed a corn-based diet.

Factory Farming (AKA Feedlot or Conventional): The process of raising farm animals in confinement at high stocking density, where a farm operates as a factory, a practice typical of corporate industrial farming. The goal is to produce the highest output at the lowest cost and antibiotics must be used to mitigate the spread of disease. Many other risks and moral issues exist as well.

Flexitarian: Refers to an individual who is conscious of the type and quality of food they consume but is open to consuming all types of foods from vegetarian to meats, as long as the quality is high.

Free-range/Free-roaming: Refers to animals that have access to the outdoors and are not confined to cages.

Genetic Engineering: Process of transferring specific traits, or genes, from one organism to a different plant or animal.

GMO (Genetically Modified): Refers to an organism whose genetic material has been altered using genetic engineering.

Grass-Fed: Grass-fed meat or pasture-raised meat refers to meat from animals that have been raised on foraged food such as grasses, as opposed to being fed a diet of grain-based food.

Grass-Fed/Grain-Finished: Refers to meat from animals that have been raised on grass, but given a diet of grain near the end of their life in order to fatten them up for market.

Grass-Fed/Grain-Supplemented: Refers to meat from animals that have been raised on grass but fed grain throughout their life in a controlled amount.

Heritage Foods: Heritage Foods are derived from rare and endangered breeds of livestock. Animals tend to be purebred species near extinction, and the method of production used saves the breeds and preserves genetic diversity. The organization Heritage Foods USA exists to accomplish this goal by selling foods from small farms to consumers and wholesale accounts building demand for these animals.

Macrobiotic: Refers to a holistic philosophy of living that originated in Japan and focuses on balance. The diet associated with the lifestyle is a strict whole foods pesco-vegetarian (includes fish but no meat or poultry or dairy) approach, with an emphasis on grains and Japanese foods.

Niman Ranch: A ranch and network of over 600 independent farmers and ranchers all committed to raising their animals sustainably and free of hormones and antibiotics with 100% vegetarian feeds.

Organic: When referring to produce, "organic" means the crop has been grown, packaged and shipped without the use of synthetic pesticides or fertilizers and are non-GMO (non-genetically modified). When referring to animals it means the animal was raised without the use of hormones or added antibiotics and fed only organic vegetarian feed (no animal by-products).

Pasture Raised: Pasture Raised or Grass-fed Meat refers to meat from animals that have been raised on foraged food such as grasses, as opposed to being fed a diet of grain-based food.

Pescatarian: Refers to an individual who consumes primarily a vegetarian diet with the addition of fish.

Raw Foodist: Refers to an individual who consumes a diet of only raw foods (foods not heated above 118 degrees faranheit).

Satur Farms: A local, Long Island-based family owned farm that specializes in growing vegetables and culinary ingredients. Although not certified organic, they are committed to organic standards.

Seasonal: Refers to the practice of eating or serving foods that are grown during that particular season.

Seitan: Often used by vegetarians as a meat substitute for its similar texture and high protein content, it is actually the gluten from wheat boiled in a ginger soy sauce.

Sustainably Raised: Refers to a food (animal or produce) that has been created in a way that has minimal negative impact on the environment.

Tempeh: A food derived from fermenting soybeans and pressing them into cakes.

Tofu: A food made from soybeans, water and a coagulant or curdling agent.

Vegan: Refers to an individual who will not consume any foods derived from an animal.

Vegetarian: Refers to an individual who will not eat any foods derived from an animal except for dairy and eggs, since it was not necessary to kill the animal to obtain the food.

Vegetarian Feed: Refers to the diet fed to an animal. It means the animal has not been fed any animal by-products and is usually fed a diet of corn or other grains, but not grass.

APPENDICES

Naturally Sweetened Desserts

Fine Dining

When you are in a Hurry (Fast Food)

Don't Forget To Register Your Purchase

Go to cleanplatesnyc.com now and register your purchase using code: imhealthy and receive six months free access to our searchable online database of restaurants plus many other benefits described below.

We are building a community and a resource for all your needs related to dining healthier!

Once you are registered you will begin to enjoy the many benefits of *Clean Plates NYC*. Here are just a few...

- An online database of all the restaurants including multiple search options
- Receive notification of new openings and closings
- Have access to the *Clean Plates NYC* Forum where you can join others sharing information and opinions on the restaurants and eating healthier
- Receive special offers and promotional programs specifically designed for *Clean Plates NYC*
- Participate in educational tele-seminars and other events with Jared and guest speakers ranging from the top chefs in Manhattan to nationally known nutrition and health experts

Further Your Education

Interested in the material in *Clean Plates NYC* and want to take it further? Here are some options...

- Personalized Counseling: Set up an initial one-on-one nutrition and wellness consultation either over the phone or in person in Manhattan or New Jersey. Custom Programs are available to meet your needs and goals.
- Group Options: Create a custom group program or have Jared speak at your company or event.
- Get Certified: For an exciting career and to enhance your personal growth, I highly recommend the Institute for Integrative Nutrition with live classes in Manhattan (integrativenutrition.com). Their life-changing Professional Training Program includes world-renowned guest speakers and a community of people dedicated to making the world a healthier, happier place. Mention *Clean Plates NYC* to receive a discount on tuition.

Contact: jared@cleanplatesnyc.com

Give the Gift of Clean Plates

Show you care! Not only will you contribute to the health and dining enjoyment of someone you care about, but you will also be contributing to charities dedicated to finding cures or preventing certain diseases like Breast Cancer and protecting and healing our planet. *Clean Plates NYC* is committed to sharing a significant portion of its proceeds with different charities.

Clean Plates NYC is the perfect gift for your family, friends, coworkers, employees, or clients.

Want to buy multiple copies for your whole company or as a promotional item for your clients? Contact Jared to find out about special pricing or for help creating a custom program.

Contact: jared@cleanplatesnyc.com

NOTES

PRAISE FOR CLEAN PLATES

"Jared's nutritional advice in Clean Plates has the power to transform your individual health and our collective well-being."
–Deepak Chopra, M.D.

"Knowledge is power, and awareness is the first step in healing. Clean Plates NYC is a highly valuable source of information that can empower you to make informed and intelligent choices about where to eat in New York."
–Dean Ornish, M.D., Clinical Professor of Medicine, University of California, San Francisco. Bestselling author of *Eat More, Weigh Less* and *The Spectrum*

"There should be a 'Clean Plates' for every city in the country! An invaluable resource to help you navigate to real food in a toxic nutritional wasteland."
–Mark Hyman, M.D., NY Times bestselling author of *UltraMetabolism* and *UltraPrevention*,

"Hurray for Clean Plates NYC—a quick, thorough, and easy way to eat well in The Big Apple." –Christiane Northrup, M.D., bestselling author of *Women's Bodies, Women's Wisdom*

"A cute compact volume in Tiffany blue dedicated to culling New York's best healthy, sustainable restaurants...It's less preachy than practical...an ideal gift for someone trying to make a positive change in their diet, and a useful one for any foodie looking for better ways to eat and to live."
–Andrea Strong of The Strong Buzz

"This is the best guide to healthy eating at the most delicious places in NYC"
–Mariel Hemingway, Academy Award nominated actress

"The most comprehensive pocket guide I have ever read. Not only will you learn where to dine, but how to make healthy choices for yourself and the planet. Please create one for every city."
–Kris Carr, bestselling author, filmmaker of *Crazy Sexy Cancer*